T5-AQQ-639

The Impeachment Of

Jim Ferguson

JIM FERGUSON, a small-town banker, was elected governor of Texas in 1914 on a promise to enact a law that would limit the rent that landowners could charge tenant farmers. He adopted the nickname "Farmer Jim" and was revered by a generation of Texans as the Champion of the Tenant Farmer.

— *Photo from Texas State Library*

The Impeachment Of
Jim
Ferguson

Bruce Rutherford

EAKIN PRESS   AUSTIN, TEXAS

FIRST EDITION

Copyright © 1983
By Bruce Rutherford

Published in the United States of America
By Eakin Press, P.O. Box 23066, Austin, Texas 78735

ISBN 0-89015-386-8

ii

In memory of my parents

Bill and Fran Rutherford

ACKNOWLEDGMENTS

I am indebted to many friendly and helpful people at the Temple Public Library, Fort Worth Public Library, and the Mary Couts Burnett Library at Texas Christian University.

Karen Warren of the Austin Travis County Collection was very helpful in obtaining photographs as was Michael Dabrishus of the Texas State Library.

Ed Eakin read an earlier manuscript of this book and offered many suggestions for its improvement. Shortcomings which remain are the fault of the author.

My wife, Sharon, and our children, Laurie, and Jason, offered support and encouragement for which I will always be grateful.

BRUCE RUTHERFORD

TABLE OF CONTENTS

Introduction vii

1 The Call of the Speaker 1
2 The Unknown Ferguson 15
3 The Proceedings of the House 23
4 The High Court of Impeachment 71
5 The Acting Governor 115
6 Jim Ferguson and the Ku Klux Klan 121
7 Jim Ferguson and Richard Nixon:
       The Constitutional Questions 133
8 Jim Ferguson and Lyndon Johnson:
       The Meaning of a Legend 141

Notes 147
Bibliography 151

FARMER JIM FERGUSON. From a portrait painting.
— *Photo from Texas State Library*

INTRODUCTION

The Texas legislature impeached and convicted Governor Jim Ferguson in the summer of 1917, and the Texas Senate imposed a stern penalty: it forbade Ferguson from ever holding office under Texas jurisdiction again. His impeachment, however, was only a milestone in Jim Ferguson's career. Ignoring the judgment of the Texas Senate, he proceeded to run again for governor, for U.S. senator and for president of the United States on his own Independent Party ticket. He lost three successive elections. In 1924 he attempted to run again for governor of Texas, but the Texas courts finally upheld the judgment of the High Court of Impeachment, and his name was omitted from the ballot. Ferguson then installed his wife as a stand-in candidate, and Mrs. Ferguson became the first and only woman to be elected governor of Texas. Ferguson claimed that his name had been vindicated; he had reclaimed what had wrongfully been taken from him.

It is because of Jim Ferguson's later career that the story of his impeachment has fallen into obscurity. Farmer Jim Ferguson is remembered as the Champion of the Tenant Farmer and the nemesis of the Ku Klux Klan; he and his wife are remembered as Ma and Pa Ferguson, and thought of as something of a comedy duo. But the important matter of Ferguson's impeachment — the reasons for it and the circumstances under which it was effected — are generally unknown, even among people who have been educated at Texas universities.

And yet the impeachment of Jim Ferguson is a momentous event in Texas legal history as well as political history, and it is very important in American legal history. It is important in Texas history because the question of Ferguson's impeachment dominated Texas politics between the World Wars. It is important in the broader field of American legal history because of the precedents that it sets and the questions that it answers. For all of the issues that baffle legal scholars — Is impeachment a criminal or a civil proceeding? What constitutes an impeachable offense? Is impeachment subject to judicial review? — are met and answered in the case of Jim Ferguson. There is no doubt that the impeachment of Governor Ferguson contributed in a significant way to the law of impeachment; and indeed, the Texas episode of 1917 provides a classic model case for the study of impeachment.

Further, the impeachment of Jim Ferguson offers a strong parallel with the process that was begun against President Richard Nixon; a study of the Ferguson affair even offers some insight into what might have transpired if Richard Nixon had not resigned.

Finally, the impeachment of Jim Ferguson directly affected the life of Lyndon Johnson, for it brought Johnson's father back into Texas politics. And Jim Ferguson strongly influenced the life of Lyndon Johnson in a way that is not yet fully appreciated but is explained in this study.

Most of the material for this book was obtained from daily newspaper reports at the time in question. Specifically, I have relied heavily on the *Temple Daily Telegram* of 1917 and 1924. Temple, Texas, was Jim Ferguson's hometown and the *Daily Telegram* was an important paper in Texas during that period. It offered the full wire service accounts of the proceedings in the Texas capitol as well as additional insights that could only have come from the local level and from Ferguson's home.

Because so much of the material was taken from this source, I have decided not to insert footnotes in the text of the book. To do so would have been hopelessly repetitive. Other sources, of course, were invaluable to me, and they are detailed in the section of Notes.

Three items of interest must be mentioned. Many of the characters in this story were known by their initials — Ferguson was prosecuted by M. M. Crane and defended by W. A. Hanger. They are identifed by their initials in this book. Second, a great many sums of money are mentioned in the story, and in every instance, I have dropped the cents and used only the dollar figure. Finally, it must be emphasized that Jim Ferguson's bank, the Temple State Bank, a centerpiece of controversy, no longer exists and should not be confused with any bank now doing business in Temple, Texas.

During his political oblivion, from 1917 to 1924, Farmer Jim lived in Temple and published a sporadic Populist newspaper, *The Ferguson Forum*. It served as his personal media link to the voters of Texas.

— *Photo from Austin-Travis County Collection*

1

The Call of the Speaker

On July 23, 1917, the speaker of the Texas House of Representatives, F. O. Fuller, issued a call for a special session of the Texas legislature to convene August 1, to consider impeaching the governor of Texas, James Edward Ferguson. Speaker Fuller's call was in some ways logical, for public sentiment had certainly been rising against the second-term governor, but in one regard his call was questionable: For on the face of it, it appeared to be unconstitutional; only the governor of Texas has the power to call a special session of the legislature.

"Farmer Jim" Ferguson had come to power in the election of 1914 from the presidency of the Temple State Bank, a small bank in a small town in a cotton-growing district in Central Texas, north of Austin. Charges had been made that as governor Ferguson had diverted state funds to the Temple State Bank and had browbeaten the officers of the bank into lending him excessively large sums of money. Other charges had accused the governor of misusing the funds that had been appropriated for lights and fuel at the governor's mansion. In March of 1917 a House investigating committee had looked into Ferguson's financial dealings and condemned him for misconduct; but the committee had determined that Ferguson's questionable dealings did not warrant an impeachment.

During the same period, though, Ferguson had conducted a bitter feud with the University of Texas. For reasons that are still not clear, he had demanded that the Board of Regents fire certain professors at the university; he had attempted to stack the Board of Regents with friends who would fire the professors to whom he objected; and he had called for the resignation of the university's president.

On May 28, while Ferguson was holding a meeting of the Regents in his office in the capitol building, students from the university paraded from the campus to the capitol and staged a protest rally in front of Ferguson's office. They came with their marching band and carrying signs, such as ''Down with Kaiserism at home,'' and speakers began to lambast Ferguson's conduct toward the university.

Ferguson was enraged by the student demonstrators; he got involved in a yelling match with one of the speakers, and even had to be restrained from climbing out his window to fight the students. The meeting of the Board of Regents was dissolved. Ferguson was convinced that the protest had been instigated by the university's president, Robert Vinson, and he now decided that Vinson simply must resign, or the governor could not approve the university's appropriation for the coming year. Vinson declined to offer his resignation, and a few days later, on June 3, Ferguson vetoed the entire university appropriation, except for the salary of one administrator of the College of Mines.

After his veto of the university appropriation, the University of Texas Ex-Students Association began to press for Jim Ferguson's impeachment. It is difficult to overstate the importance of the Ex-Students Association in the Ferguson affair, for the group had significant political influence in Texas, and during June and July the Ex-Students took out advertisements in most of the newspapers in Texas, calling for the removal of the governor.

Now in addition to his financial dealings and his apparent vendetta against the University of Texas, Governor Ferguson had become embroiled in a third controversy, which involved none other than speaker of the House.

Governor Ferguson, Speaker Fuller, Lieutenant Governor Hobby and two other men had been appointed by the previous legislature to serve as a locating board to select a site for the newly created West Texas A. and M. University. The men toured West Texas, visiting several cities that wanted the new college, and later met in Austin to vote on a site; they awarded the school to Abilene. Afterward, however, three members of the board re-

"Ma and Pa" Ferguson among friends, the common people of Texas, on one of their last hurrahs in Austin.
— *Austin-Travis County Collection*

vealed to reporters that they had not voted for Abilene, and Speaker Fuller attempted to persuade Ferguson to reconvene the board. But the two men held a private meeting, and Ferguson persuaded the speaker to let the matter drop and to even sign a statement saying that the voting had been fair and accurate.

On July 23 Fuller renounced the statement. Both he and Lieutenant Governor Hobby released sworn affidavits to the press in Houston, Fuller charging that Ferguson had duped him and had probably rigged the voting. Hobby's affidavit said simply that he had not voted for Abilene and had acted on the advice of the governor in letting the matter drop. At the same time Fuller released his affidavit, he issued his call for a special session of the legislature. The call emphasized the matter of the university appropriation:

> The University of Texas cannot be maintained on the salary of one man. He has said the university cannot open its doors until the faculty members he objects to are expelled. He has called the faculty grafters and liars without reason. He has sought to substitute his will for the will of the Board of Regents, demanding that members of the faculty be dismissed without a hearing. He has removed regents without good cause.

After Fuller released his call for a special session, the question was whether the Texas legislators would respond to it. Fuller did not have the constitutional authority to call a special session, and Jim Ferguson's supporters insisted that the legislature could not convene without a call by Ferguson.

In the two days following Fuller's call, Ferguson refused to make any comments. On July 26, however, he gave a speech to the State Farmers Institute meeting in Austin, responding to the charges and attacking. Was it fair for the university to carry dead men on the payroll? he asked. No, and Jim Ferguson was going to camp on their trails for as long as he was governor, he said, and what was more, he could be governor for as long as he wanted. As for Fuller, Ferguson had seen the speaker vote for Abilene.

There the issue stood. Fuller had issued a call for a special session and Ferguson had attacked the speaker in a retalitory speech. No one knew if the Texas legislature would convene for a special session or not. A conference of lawyers meeting in Austin on the same day Ferguson addressed the Farmers Institute released a statement saying that the call of the speaker was indeed constitutional, that the House of Representatives was capable of executing any power granted it by the constitution, and that since the House had to assemble in order to impeach, it could in fact assemble whenever it needed to in order to impeach. But that conference of lawyers was no doubt comprised of Ferguson opponents, and the statement had little impact.

The next day, however, a more serious blow fell upon the beleaguered governor. The Travis County Grand Jury, which had been investigating Ferguson's financial dealings, indicted him on criminal charges. (Travis County is the seat of Austin, the state capital.) The charges included seven counts of misapplication of funds, one count of diversion of a special fund, and most serious, one count of embezzlement.

The charges of misapplication of funds dealt mostly with money from a fire insurance settlement the state had received after a fire destroyed the Canyon City Normal College. The settlement, which amounted to $101,356, had been received by Ferguson's predecessor, Governor Oscar B. Colquitt, who had passed the money along to Ferguson. Ferguson had supposedly deposited the money in the Temple State Bank, in which he was still a major stockholder.

The charge of diverson of a special fund concerned Ferguson's use of the mansion appropriation to buy personal items, and the crucial charge of embezzlement was based on a loan repayment Ferguson had made with funds in his governor's account in the Temple State Bank, the amount in question being $5,600.

The grand jury also indicted the secretary of state, the state banking commissioner and the superintendent of public buildings and grounds.

The Travis County sheriff served process papers to Ferguson at about six p.m., and the governor was forced to post a $13,000 bond — $5,000 on the charge of embezzlement and $1,000 on each of the other charges. That night Ferguson released a statement to the press, saying that the charges had been inspired by the same crowd that had sent the "mob" of students to intimidate him. He said he would run for governor for a third term, so that the people of Texas could decide whether the state would run the university, or the university would run the state. He explained that he had kept the Canyon City Normal insurance funds in the Temple State Bank to "keep it handy" and that every penny of the settlement had been used to rebuild the college. He welcomed the challenge and wanted "this crowd of political rapscallions to trot their fastest horse."

In effect, Ferguson wanted to put the issue to a referendum, but the next election was over a year away, and he stood little chance of postponing the issue for that long. On the same day Ferguson was indicted, the attorney general of Texas issued a statement. Attorney General Ben Looney said that he anticipated that his office would be asked to make a decision as to the legality of the call of the speaker of the House for a special session. In his opinion, said Looney, the call was indeed constitutional, considering the extreme circumstances. Almost at once Texas legislators began arriving in Austin, and it was rumored that every room in the palatial Driskill Hotel had been reserved by the forces favoring impeachment.

In fact the rooms had been reserved by Will Hogg. Hogg was the son of former Texas Governor Jim Hogg and was also the founder and leader of the University of Texas Ex-Students Association. The association has been taking out newspaper advertisements calling for Ferguson's removal, and Hogg had arranged for the transcript of the House investigating committee's proceedings to be published and distributed in Austin. Even though the committee had decided in March that Ferguson's financial dealings did not warrant an impeachment, the transcript still contained a good deal of damaging information. In addition, Hogg had met with Speaker Fuller earlier in the summer and may actually have persuaded the speaker to issue his call.

On July 28, the day after his indictment, Ferguson gave a

UNIVERSITY OF TEXAS students march to the capitol. Many of the students would soon be wearing the uniform of the U.S. Army and serve in the Great War in France.

— *Austin-Travis County Collection*

speech to a group of farmers in Walnut Springs, a small town near Ferguson's summer ranch in Bosque County. In speaking to farmers, Ferguson was addressing his true constituents; he was among friends. For Jim Ferguson had won the governorship in 1914 as a political unknown mainly on the basis of his promise to enact a tenant farm law that would limit the rent that landlords could require tenant farmers to pay. He later won passage of his Tenant Farm Law, and he would be revered by a generation of Texans as the Champion of the Tenant Farmer. And since a majority of the people of Texas were farmers, and a majority of the farmers were tenants, it is easy to see the strong basis of Ferguson's support.

On that day in 1917, Ferguson spoke to 2,000 farmers in Walnut Springs. The landscape of Texas has changed dramatically since then: the small towns of Bosque County, like those in other counties, have withered. The countryside is no longer covered with small farms, and it is safe to say that no politician will ever again attract a crowd of 2,000 people to Walnut Springs to listen to a speech.

Farmer Jim Ferguson told his listeners that day that the professors at the University of Texas were "corruptionists and butterfly chasers; they were worse than draft dodgers." As for Speaker Fuller, Ferguson had seen him vote for Abilene. He dared Fuller to look him in the eye and tell him that he had not.

The farmers were probably puzzled by Ferguson's speech that day. The papers would report that the governor spoke for two hours and that he held his listeners in close attention. That was unusual, for Farmer Jim could usually put a crowd into a frenzy. After he got warmed up, his supporters would yell, "Pour it on 'em, Jim!" But they listened quietly in Walnut Springs. There was a war on, and men from the farms were already being called into the Armed Forces. It was a strange time for the governor of Texas to wage a personal war against the University of Texas. The day after his speech, the phone company manager in Ferguson's home town resigned to accept a commission in the Signal Corps; and in Austin, unfriendly legislators had filled the Driskill Hotel.

Jim Ferguson must have known that a quorum of the House

of Representatives was present in Austin and that a special session was going to convene in answer to Speaker Fuller's call. So on July 30 he made a strategic move that complicated the constitutional question: he issued his own call for a special session of the legislature.

Following a call by the governor, a special session of the legislature would of course be entirely constitutional, except for one thing: a special session must deal only with the matter for which it is called. The governor of Texas may call for a special session of the legislature to consider a specific issue, and the legislature is prohibited from taking up other matters. Ferguson did not call for a special session to have himself impeached; he called for the legislature to consider the appropriation for the University of Texas. Not coincidentally, he called for the legislature to convene on the same day that Speaker Fuller had asked it to:

> Whereas it has been untruthfully stated and persistently circulated that I vetoed said appropriation because I knew at the time that on account of the fact that the legislature had adjourned the legislature would not have an opportunity to override my said veto;
>
> Now, therefore, by virtue of the authority vested in me under the constitution and the laws of the state of Texas, I do hereby call and convoke the Thirty-fifth legislature in a second called or special session, and order that the same be convened at the state capitol at Austin, Texas, at 12 o'clock high noon, Wednesday, the first day of August, 1917, for the purpose of considering and making additional appropriations for the support and maintenance of the state university for the two fiscal years beginning September 1, 1917, and ending August 31, 1919.

The Texas legislature did indeed convene at noon on August 1, but the question was had it convened in answer to the call of the speaker or the call of the governor? The answer came quickly. Fifteen minutes after the session opened, the speaker of the House took the podium and read a list of thirteen charges that he wished to prefer against the governor of Texas. He asked the House to investigate the charges and consider whether a bill of impeachment should be presented to the Texas Senate.

Most of Fuller's charges were based on the governor's financial dealings, as revealed in the March investigation by a House committee, and his actions toward the University of Texas. But one of Fuller's charges dealt with the location of the new college, and his final charge was a complete surprise. For Fuller now claimed that the governor had actually tried to *bribe* the speaker of the House. Jim Ferguson was sitting in the gallery and listened as Fuller read the charges against him. Briefly, these are the thirteen charges that Fuller brought against Ferguson:

1. The House investigating committee had determined that Ferguson had misapplied several thousand dollars of the mansion fund by spending the money on groceries, gasoline, and other items. Ferguson had promised to repay that money to the state but had never done so.

2. Ferguson had received over $100,00 from his predecessor, the money being the proceeds of the Canyon City Normal College fire insurance settlement. Ferguson removed the money from banks where it was drawing interest and placed it in banks where it did not. This included $40,000 that he placed in the Temple State Bank, in which he was still a 25 percent stockholder. The bank profited from the funds, and so did Ferguson.

3. Ferguson had misappropriated $5,600 by using state funds in his governor's account in the Temple State Bank to settle a personal debt. This had occurred on August 23, 1915.

4. More than $100,000 of the state's money had been kept in the Temple State Bank even though Ferguson knew that the law required the money to be kept in the state treasury.

5. Despite the fact that the banking laws forbade a bank to lend money in excess of 30 percent of its capital stock, Ferguson had induced the officers of the Temple State to lend him more than $170,000, which alone exceeded the entire capital stock of the bank.

6. Ferguson had permitted one of his appointees to draw the salary of his office despite the fact that the Texas Sen-

ate had refused to confirm the man's appointment. The appointee was C. W. Woodman, whom Ferguson had named labor commissioner. When the Senate declined to confirm Woodman, Ferguson appointed Woodman's chief deputy to fill the vacancy. But even now, since the chief deputy had failed to qualify, C. W. Woodman was still acting as commissioner and drawing the salary of the office.

7. The governor had vetoed the entire appropriation for the University of Texas, except for the salary of one officer, ignoring the mandate of the Texas constitution, which expressly provided for the support and maintenance of the University of Texas.

8. Governor Ferguson had tried to have certain University of Texas faculty members expelled, even after the Board of Regents ruled that the faculty members had done nothing to warrant their dismissal. This ignored the civil statutes that placed the management of the affairs of the University of Texas with the Board of Regents.

9. The governor had also sought to remove members of the Board of Regents without good cause. He had demanded the resignation of other regents; and his actions had been taken so that he could personally dictate to the Board as to the management of the affairs of the university.

10. Governor Ferguson had declared in public speeches and published writings that the faculty of the University of Texas was composed of grafters, corruptionists, liars, and men who were disloyal to their government. The members of the faculty had petitioned the Texas Senate to investigate the governor's charges, and the Senate had forgone the investigation only after Ferguson promised certain senators that he would not repeat the charges. But after the legislature had adjourned, Ferguson had indeed repeated and intensified the charges. This, according to the speaker of the House, constituted criminal libel against the fair name of Texas.

11. Ferguson had refused to reconvene the committee appointed to locate the West Texas A. and M. College, even though three of the five members of the committee had signed

affidavits that they had not voted for Abilene, the city to which the new college had been awarded.

12. The governor had remanded a $5,000 bail bond to Wilbur P. Allen, the chairman of the University of Texas Board of Regents. Ferguson remanded the bond to Allen only in an attempt to influence Allen's actions as a member of the Board of Regents.

13. Finally, Fuller claimed that Ferguson had sought to influence him by offering him a long-term, low-interest loan, which Fuller did not even have to repay if he did not want to. Fuller suspected Ferguson's motives, and for that reason he accepted the money from Ferguson—$100 in cash and a check for $400, all of which Fuller had kept and would exhibit to the House of Representatives.

Fuller's charges of course created a stir on the floor of the House and in the gallery as well. No move was made to act on the charges that day—time was running short—but Ferguson's supporters made one tactical move. They introduced a resolution calling for a committee of both the House and Senate to fully investigate the management of the University of Texas. The resolution was ruled out of order, as the Senate was not then in session, a quorum having not yet arrived in Austin. A decision as to whether the House would take up the speaker's allegations was put off until tomorrow.

That evening Ferguson defended his loan to Speaker Fuller: He had loaned Fuller the money as a friend. Fuller had come to him and asked him for help. If Ferguson had been attempting to influence anyone, he asked, would he have given his personal check for $400 and also have kept Fuller's note? Of course not, he said.

The next day, the issue was decided. The House determined by a vote of 83 to 41 to investigate Speaker Fuller's charges against the governor and decide whether a bill of impeachment should be presented to the Texas Senate. Ferguson supporters called for the installation of a temporary speaker, but the proposal was voted down. The House agreed, however, that Fuller would appoint a chairman to preside while the House took up the matter as a Committee of the Whole. The House also decided to appoint an attorney to rule on the admissability of evidence. Ferguson backers sought to delay the proceedings until a report from the rules committee could be obtained, but that effort also failed.

The following day, Friday, August 3, the appointments were made. Representative Fly, who had chaired the House investigating committee in March, was named chairman of the Committee of the Whole; Representative Bryan was appointed to decide on the admissability of evidence. The House would hire M. M. Crane to serve as its legal counsel; Ferguson announced that he would be represented by W. A. Hanger. After the appointments had been made, the House adjourned until Monday in order for process to be served.

The proceedings against Jim Ferguson were, in one sense, a contest between the governor and the speaker of the House, but in another sense they were simply a contest between two great Texas attorneys — M. M. Crane and W. A. Hanger.

M. M. Crane had served as a state legislator and state senator, as lieutenant governor and as Texas attorney general. He had served as attorney general in the 1890s, during the reign of the progressive Governor James Stephen Hogg, and had won national fame for his prosecution of anti-trust cases. After an unsuccessful run for governor, he left public office at the turn of the century and took up private legal practice in Dallas. At age 62, he was probably the most respected lawyer in Texas, when the House investigating committee called on him to serve as its counsel in the March proceedings concerning Governor Ferguson's financial dealings. Crane had grilled Ferguson on the witness stand during those proceedings, and he was now as familiar with Jim Ferguson's finances as the governor's own bookkeeper. His appointment for the impeachment deliberations did not bode well for the governor.

W. A. Hanger was also a former state senator, and a political leader in Tarrant County. He was a widely known trial lawyer and was now, at age 49, a partner in the most prestigious law firm in Fort Worth. Hanger had obtained his law degree at Cumberland College in Lebanon, Tennessee. Surprisingly enough, that was an impressive credential for a Texas lawyer in the nineteenth century.

Before the rise of Texas law schools, it was almost customary for an ambitious young man to return to one of the old southern states to obtain his legal education. Perhaps it is because Sam Houston himself once practiced law in Lebanon that Cumberland became an educational Mecca for young Texans. At any rate, the tradition continued into the twentieth century. Jimmy Allred, who served as governor of Texas in the 1930s, was a graduate of Cumberland, as was Lyndon Johnson's brother, Sam Houston. And Cumberland was proud enough of its alumnus W. A. Hanger that it awarded him an honorary Doctor of Law degree late in his life.

Hanger was known as a shrewd trial lawyer, a country boy, a cunning backwoods attorney — the ideal man, perhaps, to defend Farmer Jim.

Regardless of the outcome, Hanger and Crane would journey to Austin to face each other in a legal proceeding that had already set one constitutional precedent: For despite Jim Ferguson's own belated call, it was evident that the Texas House of Representatives had in fact convened in answer to the call of the speaker of the House.

2

The Unknown Ferguson

If Texas voters had known more about Jim Ferguson when he ran for governor in 1914, they might have been able to predict that he would get into trouble if he won the office. The way Farmer Jim told the story of his life, he was just a poor boy who worked his way up in the world, but there was more to it than that. His life had taken some funny turns long before he ran for governor.

Jim Ferguson was poor alright, growing up on the black prairie in Bell County, but he did not remain poor. Bell County grew and prospered, and young Jim Ferguson prospered along with it. In a sense, the course of the county's history set the course of Ferguson's life.

The county itself was an empty stretch of blackland prairie until 1850; by then there were just enough settlers in the area to make them believe that they deserved their own county, so the older Milam County was divided, and its western sector was made a new county. It was surveyed in 1850; an election was held; and the new county was named for the incumbent governor of Texas, Peter Hansborough Bell. A county seat was established and named Nolanville, but two years later the name was changed to Belton.

Most of the settlers in the new county, many of whom had come from the southern states of Georgia, Tennessee, and the Carolinas, lived on small farms along the banks of the Little River or the numerous creeks in the area. The settlers did not believe that the prairie would support crops — the land was too dry — and no one dreamed that you could grow cotton on it.

Happier days—Jim Ferguson delivers his inaugural address to the Texas Legislature. Texas Supreme Court Chief Justice John Nelson Phillips is seated at the rostrum behind Ferguson. After Ferguson was impeached, the Texas Senate invited Phillips to come to Austin to swear-in the Senate as a High Court of Impeachment, contacting him in North Texas by long-distance telephone (a newsworthy event in 1917). But Phillips arrived in Austin one day late, thus delaying the start of Ferguson's trial.

— *Photo from Austin-Travis County Collection,*
Austin Public Library

Close to the river, they grew wheat, sorghum, potatoes. They built a couple of mills. And they founded a college in Salado, in the southern tip of the county, in 1859. Salado College, long ago abandoned and now in ruins, became known as the "Athens of Texas."

By 1860, the population of Bell County had grown to about 4,000 white men, and a lesser but uncertain number of black men. The population might have grown more, had it not been for a drought that lasted most of the decade and made it hard for the transplanted Southerners to scrape out a living. The Civil War did not help matters.

Bell County's two delegates to the Texas secession convention voted in favor of the secession, and the ordinance to secede was passed by county voters, 495 to 198. During the war, more than 1,000 men from Bell County served in the Confederate forces; ten companies were recruited in Belton. A memorial to the Confederate dead stands today in front of the courthouse in Belton, and the public library there holds a sizable collection of decaying Confederate military records. One of the Bell County Confederate companies was commanded by Judge X. B. Saunders, who would later play a role in Jim Ferguson's career.

After the war, Federal troops were garrisoned in Belton, and the county was goverened by a radical reconstruction Commissioner's Court. The offical government policy was to confiscate everything that had belonged to the Confederate nation or had been captured from the United States. The officer commanding the troops in Belton, a lieutenant of the First Iowa Volunteer Cavalry, interpreted the policy liberally and seized every mule and wagon that had ever belonged to anyone who served in the Confederacy. Conditions grew harsh.

County residents finally regained control of the local government, and in 1871 they appointed a committee to audit the county books to see what damage had been done by the radicals. Serving on that committee was the Methodist parson, James Eldridge Ferguson. The Reverend Ferguson had settled in Bell County after the war, during which he too had commanded a company of Confederate troops.

Parson Ferguson owned a farm as well as a mill on Salado

Creek, south of Belton. On August 31, 1871, the parson's wife, Fanny, gave birth to their fourth surviving child, James Edward. Mrs. Ferguson had a fifth child when Jim was three years old; the next year, when Jim was four, Reverend Ferguson died, leaving his widow to raise the five children alone.

There was disagreement about the ownership of the mill on Salado Creek, for the minister had originally had a partner in the mill. After Parson Ferguson died, his former partner attempted to claim the mill, but two Ferguson cousins held the man off at gunpoint, then raced on horseback to Belton, where Judge X. B. Saunders looked over the legal documents and ruled that the widow Ferguson was entitled to keep the mill. The details of the story are hazy and perhaps overly dramatic; we are told of them in a book by Jim Ferguson's daughter, Ouida.

Ferguson's daughter tells us too that young Jim Ferguson entered school in Bell County, studied the McGuffey Readers, and then, at the age of twelve, entered Salado College. The college served as a boarding school as well as an institution of higher learning. There, young Ferguson studied Latin, literature, mathematics, and history. He was expelled at the age of sixteen over his refusal to cut firewood for the schoolmaster. He declined an offer to re-enroll, and instead he shortly thereafter disappeared from Bell County; he had set out for the Far West.

It is difficult to assess the amount of quality of education that Jim Ferguson possessed when he left Salado College. Dozens of Texas History books maintain that he had little formal schooling and that this is the cause of his hostility toward the University of Texas: He was envious of men of higher learning. That thesis does not seem to bear scrutiny, though, for Ferguson did have as much education as most of his contemporaries in public life. It is not known how far he was from a degree — Salado College did grant degrees — but age sixteen would not have been too young to graduate from college during that era.

From Bell County, young Ferguson worked his way west, to Denver and San Francisco, then into the Washington Territory. He worked as a miner, a lumberjack, and dishwasher. After two years in the West, he worked his way back to Texas, where he went to work for the Kansas and Texas (KATY) Railroad. He advanced to a foreman's job and worked for the line in North Texas, around Dennison and McKinney, where the line entered the Indian Territory (later the Oklahoma Territory).

In 1895, at age twenty-four, Ferguson quit the railroad and returned home to Bell County. There he helped his mother farm cotton and also took up the study of law. There is no record of Ferguson studying under the tutelage of an attorney — the customary way for a young man to enter the legal profession — but supposedly Judge X. B. Saunders helped him to become a lawyer. Ferguson's daughter says that three attorneys were appointed to examine Ferguson for admission to the bar, and one of the attorneys happened to be Judge Saunders. The judge is said to have told his colleagues that it would be unappreciative of an old friend (the late Reverend Ferguson) to subject his son to a grueling examination. So instead they sent young Ferguson out for a bottle of whiskey. Thus Jim Ferguson is supposed to have been admitted to the bar of Texas without having to answer a single question.

While studying law, Ferguson also became involved with Salado College again, taking part in debates of the Salado Debating Society. After gaining admission to the bar in 1897, he opened a law office in Belton. And at the same time, he began courting the young woman who would become his wife, Miriam Amanda Wallace.

Miss Wallace was a Bell County girl who had studied at Salado College and at Baylor Female College in Belton. She was the daughter of a wealthy widow, and Jim Ferguson's daughter maintains that their courtship was a case of poor boy marrying rich girl. In fact Miriam Amanda Wallace was of the same social class as Jim Ferguson and was practically his cousin.

Reverend Ferguson, as mentioned earlier, served in the Confederacy during the Civil War, but his brother, Wesley, fought on the side of the Union. During the war, the Ferguson brothers disavowed each other and even wished each other dead. After the war, though, they both settled in Bell County.

Brother Wesley died, leaving a widow, who later married a man named Wallace. Wesley's widow and her new husband had a daughter in 1875, and this is the girl Jim Ferguson eventually

MIRIAM FERGUSON ran as her husband's stand-in candidate for governor in 1924. Once in office, however, she was more than a figurehead. She worked in the governor's office and had a voice in the affairs of the state of Texas. She was literally a co-governor.

Campaigning against the Ku Klux Klan in 1924, she promised to "take the sheets and put them back on the beds and put the pillowcases back on the pillows, where they belong." It is a promise she kept when she signed the Anti-Mask Law in 1925.

— Photo from Texas State Library

married. The man Wallace died in 1898, leaving his widow with a small fortune in land and money. After his death, the widow began to rely on her nephew, or former nephew, the young lawyer Ferguson, for advice and counsel. And at the same time Ferguson began his courtship of Miriam Wallace. They were married on the eve of the twentieth century, December 31, 1899, in the Episcopal Church in Belton.

Jim Ferguson might have remained a small-town lawyer the rest of his life, for he was soon well established as a lawyer in Belton, and his family was happy there. He and his wife had two daughters, one born in 1900 and the second in 1903. But Jim Ferguson left the law, and partly because his life was directly affected by the history of the county he lived in.

Sometime after the birth of his first daughter, Ferguson opened a savings and loan association, in an office adjacent to the Belton Opera House, and proceeded to both practice law and operate the new business. In the winter 1904, however, a fire destroyed the opera house and gutted Ferguson's office. Ferguson's daughter later wrote that Ferguson owned the opera house and that he lost both it and his office. Actually, the Belton Opera House was a public building, and Jim Ferguson did not own it.

His daughter also wrote that Ferguson lost a law library worth over $6,000, but because of insurance prohibitions against theaters, he was only able to collect $2,000 in settlement. This is one of the mysterious events. The documents that would clarify this matter do not exist, because the Bell County Courthouse was also destroyed by fire early in the twentieth century. But we know for certain that the Belton Opera House was built for a total cost of less than $1,000. And since that is the case, it seems inconceivable that Jim Ferguson's office and books could have been worth even half that amount. Soon after he collected the fire insurance settlement, Jim Ferguson opened the Farmers State Bank in Belton, with himself as president. His pursuit of the law was now abandoned.

Bell County by this time had changed dramatically from what it had been when Jim Ferguson left Salado College to roam the West. For one thing, Bell County men had learned after the

Civil War that you could indeed grow cotton on the blackland prairies. And for another thing, the railroads had come.

In 1881, the Gulf, Colorado and Santa Fe Railroad, laying track from Houston up through Texas, reached a point where a railhead and junction was needed. Turning down an offer from the citizens of Belton, the railroad instead established its railhead a few miles east and laid out a new town. Lots in the new town were sold on June 29 of that year, and the town was named for the superintendent of the construction crew, Bernard Moore Temple. The next year, another line, the KATY, laid track through the new town. From then on, Temple, Texas, which had not existed when Jim Ferguson was a boy, was the most important town in Bell County. By 1900, its population was greater than Belton's, and it was the commerical center of the county. In 1906, Ferguson sold the Farmers State Bank and moved his family to Temple, where he opened a new, larger bank, the Temple State Bank, once again with himself as president.

Jim Ferguson was apparently successful in Temple. He built a fine two-story Victorian home, which still stands, although sadly in disrepair, and bought a ranch in neighboring Bosque County. He ran the bank in Temple until 1914, when at the age of 42, he decided to run for governor of Texas.

Jim Ferguson barnstormed Texas in 1914, calling himself Farmer Jim and promising a tenant farm law, promising to veto any liquor legislation, whether wet or dry, speaking to larger and larger crowds. And he won the election. And he kept his promises. He vetoed the legislation calling for yet another liquor referendum; he won passage of the tenant farm law. He dispatched the Texas National Guard to the Mexican border during the Pancho Villa crisis, and he attended the 1916 National Democratic Convention, where he delivered a speech in support of the minority plank opposing women's suffrage.

He was considered a handsome man — six feet tall, brown haired, having a high brow, a strong nose, feminine lips. He always wore three-piece banker's suits and is remembered as the greatest of the Texas political orators. He might have gone on to achieve national office like his contemporary, Governor Coolidge of Massachusettes; but unfortunately Farmer Jim got himself into trouble and ran into M. M. Crane.

3

The Proceedings of the House

On Monday, August 6, the silver-haired dean of Texas attorneys began the investigation into the charges preferred by Speaker Fuller. M. M. Crane called his first witness, the governor of Texas himself, James Edward Ferguson.

Through his attorney, W. A. Hanger, Jim Ferguson respectfully declined to take the stand. The governor would wait, said Hanger, and rest on his constitutional right to first hear the evidence against him. Crane pressed the matter: This was not a criminal proceeding, and the strict rules of a court of law did not apply. Jim Ferguson owed it to his colleagues to cooperate. Ferguson again declined to testify, and Crane asked Representative Bryan to make his first ruling: Could the governor of Texas refuse to take the stand? Bryan considered the question and then answered. Yes, the governor did have that constitutional right; Crane would have to begin with a different first witness.

Crane protested that this threw his plans into disarray. He would have to ask for a delay so that he could interview other witnesses and alter his plans. The House adjourned until three o'clock; when it met again, Crane called his new first witness, the assistant cashier of the Temple State Bank, Henry Blum.

Crane asked Blum to explain the circumstances of a $5,600 charge to the governor's account in the bank on August 23, 1916. (This is the money Fuller had accused Ferguson of embezzling.) Blum could only remember that there had been a mistake in the balances; he could not recall any of the details. Had there not been a payment from the governor's account to the First National Bank of Temple on that date? Blum couldn't re-

Texas Supreme Court Chief Justice John Nelson Phillips administers the lieutenant-governor's oath of office to Will Hobby. An ironic scene, for after Jim Ferguson was impeached, Hobby became acting governor; and after Ferguson's conviction, governor. Yet no one thought to administer the governor's oath of office to Hobby, even though the Texas constitution requires the governor to take the oath. Not until after he won another term in his own right did Hobby take the governor's oath of office—one minor point on which the Texas legislators of 1917 failed to obey the Texas constitution.

— Photo from Austin-Travis County Collection,
Austin Public Library

call that either. Did he recall if such a check had been shown to him when he was a witness before the grand jury? No, Blum could not recall.

Defense counsel Hanger cross-examined. Didn't the governor have a personal account and another special account, in addition to his governor's account, in the Temple State Bank? Yes, answered Blum.

Hanger: "I'll ask you, after stressing that probably the sum was charged to the governor's fund by error, to say what amount the governor had on deposit in his special account on August 23, 1916." Blum replied that the governor had $40 in his special account at the time.

Crane took the witness back and asked him what amount the governor had in his other account, the personal account, on August 23. Blum answered that the personal account was then overdrawn by $30,000.

Crane asked the assistant cashier to describe the deposits made by state officials in the Temple State Bank. Blum answered that the secretary of state, the state banking commmmissioner and the governor all kept accounts in the bank. He was able to read a list of balances for Crane—the state's deposits in the bank had gone over $350,000 in May, 1917. The secretary of state once deposited $250,000, and the governor made deposits of $20,000 at a time. Did the governor himself bring the deposits? Blum didn't know.

Crane: "Did anyone draw interest on these special accounts?"

Blum: "Not that I know of."

Had the bank ever carried state deposits before Mr. Ferguson's election? No. Wouldn't Blum say that the state funds had been of great benefit to the bank? No, said Blum, because the bank did not loan out the state's money. Crane had other questions, which Blum could not answer. Crane told the banker to bring more detailed records when he returned the next day; Blum promised to do so.

On cross-examination, Hanger elicited from Blum that the secretary of state's account had remained in the Temple State Bank for only a short period of time, and it had been totally accounted for. The banking commissioner's account was now closed, and the governor's account had a balance of only $1,105.

M. M. Crane's next witness was the Texas state treasurer, Jim Edwards. Crane asked the state treasurer if Governor Ferguson had ever repaid the mansion expenditures, as he had promised to do during the March investigation. No, said Edwards, the governor had not. Crane asked Edwards to explain the background of the question, and Edwards answered that the governor had used money from the mansion appropriation to buy groceries, gasoline, automobile tires, and other personal items.

On cross-examination, W. A. Hanger asked Edwards what he had done with the proceeds of the Canyon Normal School fire insurance settlement. (Edwards had been treasurer during the term of Ferguson's predecessor, Governor Colquitt, when the college burned.) Edwards replied that he had deposited it in an Austin bank. Didn't Edwards and Sam Sparks, the chairman of Canyon Normal's Board of Regents, have a $6,000 loan with the same bank? Yes, said Edwards.

Crane objected to the questioning, calling it irrelevant. Hanger responded that he was only trying to show that banking violations had occurred before Jim Ferguson had become governor. Crane countered that they weren't investigating violations that occurred before Ferguson's election, and this objection was upheld.

Crane then called the chief clerk of the Texas Supreme Court, Fred Connerly. The case involving Ferguson's mansion expenditures had become known as the "chicken salad case," and while the chicken salad case had been pending before the Texas Supreme Court, Ferguson had written a letter to the justices, pointing out that the Texas constitution authorized appropriations for the governor's mansion. Crane had Connerly read the letter, and after he had done so, Crane asked him if he had ever known of any other governor writing such a letter. No, Connerly had not.

The next day, Tuesday, Crane recalled Henry Blum to the stand. Blum had several corrections to offer. In the first place, they had all been in error yesterday when they talked about Jim Ferguson's bank balances on August 23, 1916. Ferguson was charged with using the state's money to settle a personal debt on August 23, 1915; they had been talking about the wrong year. In answer to questions from Hanger, he now reported that on the date in question Ferguson had $50 in his personal account and $16,000 in his special account. So the charge to his official governor's account could have been made in error.

Under Crane's questioning he also admitted that the state deposits in the bank had gone as high as $680,634. Crane himself took the records Blum had brought and read the sums of the banks financial condition—its assets, deposits, loans. He was able to demonstrate that the bank's loans in 1917 exceeded its entire capital and surplus.

Crane: "Were you mistaken when you said in previous testimony that the bank did not loan out state money?"

Blum: "You must remember that much of the state money was deposited in other banks."

But Crane challenged that point. The Temple State Bank drew interest on its deposits in other banks, didn't it? Yes, said Blum. Then weren't the funds of the State of Texas of benefit to the bank, and wasn't Jim Ferguson a 25 percent stockholder in the Temple State Bank? Blum still didn't think the funds had been a benefit to the bank.

Crane then called another banker to the stand. This was Henry Fox, the vice president of the Houston National Exchange Bank, who testified that the state penitentiary commission had kept funds in his bank which did not draw interest. And he had more important testimony.

Fox stated that in March, 1917, his bank had lent $37,500 each to the governor, the governor's brother, A. F. Ferguson, and the governor's secretary, J. H. Davis. At the same time, the Houston bank had an agreement with the Temple State Bank by which the Temple bank kept a sufficient balance in Houston to cover the loans. All of this had occurred at a time when Jim Ferguson was assuring members of the House investigating committee that he had settled his indebtedness to the Temple State Bank.

Crane read a bank examiner's report that described the condition of the Temple State Bank on December 26, 1916. The report revealed that the bank's directors had discussed reducing the line of credit to Jim Ferguson and had decided to place two sums of $50,000 each in other banks in order to reduce the amount of Ferguson's paper in the Temple State.

On Wednesday Crane opened by calling P. L. Downs, the president of the First National Bank of Temple. Downs described a loan that his bank had made to Jim Ferguson in 1913, which was to be repaid in $5,000 installments in 1914, 1915, and 1916. The second installment had been paid on August 21, 1915, and with interest had amounted to $5,600.

Crane then brought B. A. Cox, chief clerk to the Texas secretary of state, to the stand and had Cox read a number of the governor's official proclamations.

Cox read the governor's proclamation of the previous May 29, by which Ferguson removed S. J. Jones from the Board of Regents of the University of Texas. He read the proclamation of June 6, by which Governor Ferguson remitted the forfeiture of a $5,000 bail bond to Wilbur P. Allen, the chairman of the University of Texas Board of Regents. And he read Ferguson's veto of the bill increasing the salaries of state appellate judges. In the veto Ferguson wrote that $3,000 was enough for the judges, in view of the fact that the governor's salary was only $4,000.

Then Crane himself read a certificate written by John D. McCall, the secretary of the Texas Senate, which was dated April 10, 1915, and which advised Governor Ferguson that his nomination of C. W. Woodman for the post of labor commissioner had been rejected by the senate, but that his later nomination of Frank Swor had been confirmed.

Crane called a warrant clerk from the state comptroller's office, who testified that even then C. W. Woodman was still drawing the salary of labor commissioner, and Frank Swor, was drawing the salary of chief deputy.

With his next witnesses Crane turned the investigation toward the question of the University of Texas. He called Representative Dudley of El Paso, who described a meeting that he and El Paso's state senator had with Governor Ferguson.

Governor Ferguson had appointed a certain Dr. Lawrence to

serve on the University of Texas Board of Regents, but since neither of El Paso's legislators were familiar with the man, they went to the governor and asked him to appoint someone else. Ferguson would not change his appointment; he wanted a man who would "stand hitched," he told them, and do as Ferguson wanted in his fight with the university.

After Dudley, when the session reconvened in the afternoon, Crane called the president of the University of Texas, Robert E. Vinson.

In response to Crane, Vinson said that the chairman of the university's Board of Regents, Wilbur P. Allen, had come to Vinson and told him that if he and the school's secretary, John A. Lomax, would resign, then Ferguson would relent and sign the appropriation bill. Vinson had refused.

Crane asked the university president to describe his relationship with the governor, and Vinson did. After he was named president by the university's Board of Regents, Vinson had gone to pay a courtesy call on the governor. At that very first meeting, the governor demanded to know what Vinson was going to do about the professors to whom Ferguson objected — namely, Professors Battle, Potts, Mays, and Mather, and Secretary Lomax.

Vinson answered that he had nothing to do with the faculty for the coming year; the Board of Regents had already acted on that. Ferguson insisted that the men had to go. Vinson asked for specific charges against the men, but Ferguson answered only that he had evidence against them and would produce it at the proper time.

After that meeting, Vinson later wrote to the governor and asked him to detail his charges, so that Vinson could give them to the Board of Regents. Ferguson wrote back, accusing Vinson of "trying to raise an issue" and telling him that thereafter they would deal with each other only through the Board of Regents.

Crane now began to question Vinson about the matters for which Ferguson had been condemning the university. Ferguson had said that the university was elitist and was controlled by the Greek letter fraternities; he had said that the professors had easy work loads and were dishonest; that the faculty resented his proposed appropriation of $2 million for rural schools. And they were carrying dead men on the payroll.

Now Vinson claimed that the faculty was in favor of rural education and supported the appropriation for the rural schools. More Texas schoolteachers came from the University of Texas than from any other source. As for elitism, nearly 50 percent of the university's students supported themselves by working while they attended school. There were fraternities on the campus, but they did not discriminate against a man because of poverty or social background.

Were they carrying dead men on the payroll at the university? Absolutely not, said Vinson. He produced the list to which Ferguson had objected: the chair of sociology had never been filled; the position of assistant secretary of the university had never been filled; nor had the position of professor of clinical psychology. But these items were only in the *budget;* they were not on the *payroll.*

Hanger objected to Vinson trying to differentiate between a payroll and a budget; Vinson answered, somewhat obliquely, that no one knew exactly how much it cost to maintain the university, except God. The chair overruled Hanger's objection.

And finally, M. M. Crane said that he had heard a lot about the easy work load of university professors. Not so, said Vinson. He himself worked two eight-hour days every 24 hours, and most professors worked 39 hours a week, plus time spent in preparation and time spent on writing books.

The next day, the ninth, Vinson returned to the stand and told of a meeting of the Board of Regents at which the governor chastised two regents whom he had appointed for voting not to seat another of Ferguson's appointees. Vinson said that Ferguson lambasted Dr. Faber and W. R. Brents and even told Faber that he should resign if he couldn't obey Ferguson's wishes.

Vinson also answered new questions about fraternities at the university. Were they snobbish? No. Did they control the social life of the university? No. Besides, said Vinson, Governor Ferguson himself was an honorary member of a fraternity; this drew a round of laughter from the assembly.

W. A. Hanger then cross-examined the university president, and his questions must have seemed nitpicking and petty to the members of the House. In any event, Vinson handled the questions adroitly.

What was done with the profits of the university co-op? That was a non-profit concern, said Vinson, intended to supply materials for the students; there were no profits. What was done with the fees obtained for correspondence work? The professors who taught the courses were paid with the fees. What about the business of sending University women out to teach farmers' wives how to cook and can vegetables? The university, said Vinson, had only been following the directions of the U.S. Department of Agriculture.

Hanger grilled Vinson about the university payroll; he asked for the numbers of instructors and assistants and what their salaries were. Vinson readily supplied the answers along with facts that probably surprised his questioner.

The cost of educating a student at the University of Texas, said Vinson, was less than at most other state schools. As for the payroll, the salary for a full professor was $3,000 a year — only $100 more than it had been in 1885.

Vinson returned to the stand on Friday and told Crane that he did not know why Ferguson wanted the professors fired. He did remember that Ferguson had charged Professor Mathers with profiting from the university co-op.

Then Crane called Law Professor R. E. Coffer, who would no longer be a professor after August 31, because the Board of Regents had finally dismissed the men Ferguson had wanted fired. Coffer told Crane that Ferguson's hatred of him had begun at a political convention when they had opposed each other on a couple of issues.

Crane then recalled Henry Blum, who admitted that the Ferguson and J. H. Davis notes of $37,500 each had been sold to the Houston National Exchange Bank on March 7, 1916. The notes had been sold for a period of one month, and a bank examiner would not have been able to tell that the Temple State Bank was liable for them.

Crane: Wasn't it true that not a dollar had changed hands on that deal? Blum: Yes. The purpose of the arrangement was to reduce Ferguson's indebtedness to the Temple State Bank. While the notes were in Houston, his bank had maintained a sufficient balance at the Houston National to cover them.

Then Chester Terrell, who was acting as Speaker Fuller's personal counsel, asked where the notes had been on April 6. They were in the Temple bank on April 6, at which time Ferguson had notes of $100,000 with the bank; this included a note for $37,500 which had been loaned to the Bell-Bosque Ranch. (This was Ferguson's ranch.)

Terrell asked about the $5,600 charge to the governor's account on August 23, 1915. If the 21st had fallen on a Saturday, wouldn't a transaction for that day have been entered on the books on Monday? Yes.

Just before the noon recess, Crane had Ferguson's message vetoing the university appropriation read into the record. In that veto, Ferguson condemned the administration of President Vinson, condemned fraternities and class distinctions at the university, and said that too many people were going "hog wild over higher education."

At the opening of the afternoon session, Crane announced that counsel for both sides had agreed that August 21, 1915, was a Saturday, and August 23 was a Monday. Crane then turned to the West Texas A. and M. matter.

He began by calling Land Commissioner Davis and then Lieutenant Governor Will Hobby. Both men said that they had not voted for Abilene to get the new college. The meeting to decide the matter had been conducted in executive session, and after Abilene had won, or had appeared to win three votes, they made the decision unanimous by a voice vote. Later, Hobby, Davis and the speaker of the House had all denied to the press that they voted for Abilene, so how did Abilene get three votes?

Crane would take up that question on Monday. The members of the House were reluctant to adjourn for the weekend, preferring to meet on Saturday, but W. A. Hanger's son was said to be seriously ill in Fort Worth, and Hanger wanted to return home for the weekend. Hearing this, the House voted unanimously to adjourn until Monday.

The second week of the House proceedings began on Monday, August 13; but before it sat as a Committee of the Whole, Speaker Fuller addressed a short speech to the House.

Fuller said that he had learned that Texas Rangers and gunmen had insisted on entering the gallery armed during the hearings. (Texas Rangers, like tenant farmers, were extremely loyal to Farmer Jim, and the feeling was that the Rangers were there to protect the governor.)

"I want to protest against this," said the speaker of the House. "The chair is of the opinion that the state of Texas has reached the stage when no department of the state government needs to place an armed guard over the legislature. The chair is unarmed, and his friends are unarmed."

He added that appeals to the sergeant-at-arms and the adjutant general had been to no avail, and he wanted the members to know of the matter. Now M. M. Crane resumed the investigation.

Before returning to the matter of the college locating board, Crane again called witnesses to discuss Governor Ferguson's financial dealings. Curtiss Hancock, the chairman of the Texas Highway Commission, testified that the governor had called his attention to the fact automobile registration fees had to be turned into the state treasury only on a quarterly basis and suggested that the funds — about $1.2 million a year — be distributed among several banks, including a Temple bank. Hancock had assumed that the governor meant the Temple State Bank. He later told the other members of the commission, but they never did as the governor requested. All the commission's funds were handled through the Citizens Bank and Trust of Austin, which had been chosen on the advice of the secretary of state.

And Carl Widen, an assistant cashier of the American National Bank of Austin, testified that on May 19, 1917, $250,000 had been deposited in his bank to the credit of the secretary of state's account in the Temple State Bank. The deposit had consisted of five checks of $50,000 each.

On cross-examination, W. A. Hanger brought out that several other state agencies had collection accounts in the American National and that they were maintained there merely for convenience.

Now Crane returned to the question of the locating board and called the state land commissioner, Fred W. Davis.

Commissioner Davis, who was one of the three members who had signed affidavits that they had not voted for Abilene, now read a letter that Speaker Fuller had written to him on July 7. In the letter, Fuller said that he too had not voted for Abilene and suggested that they reconvene the locating board to settle the matter.

Cross-examining, Hanger asked Davis about a later meeting between Davis, Speaker Fuller and Governor Ferguson, at which they signed a statement that the selection of Abilene had been fair and accurate. At that meeting, asked Hanger, had the speaker of the House suggested reconvening the board? No, said Davis, he had not. Had Davis himself signed the statement? Yes, Davis admitted that he had, but only on the condition that three members of the board would not sign affidavits that they had not voted for Abilene. He had made that reservation when he signed the statement.

Crane called the attorney general of Texas, Ben. F. Looney. The attorney general testified that when the locating board met, Speaker Fuller had already told him that he opposed granting the college to Abilene because of its poor water supply.

On cross-examination, Hanger asked Looney if even then he and Fuller had discussed impeaching the governor. Yes. And he admitted that he had talked about it with others, including the leader of the University of Texas Ex-Students Association, Will Hogg.

That afternoon Crane called Speaker Fuller to the stand, but turned him over to his personal counsel, Chester Terrell, for questioning. Fuller told his story.

Fuller said that he toured the West Texas cities that desired the new college, along with the other members of the board, including the governor, although the lieutenant governor had not been with them. Fuller had favored Haskell or Snyder to get the school and told the governor so.

After the tour, Fuller came to Austin on June 27; Lieutenant Governor Hobby arrived on the 28th. On June 29, they met with the governor, and they all agreed to convene the board the next day.

The next morning a Texas Ranger notified Fuller that the governor wanted to see him, so Fuller went to the capitol and met Ferguson.

Ferguson told Fuller that he wanted Fuller to stand by him on this A. and M. matter, and if Fuller would do so, Ferguson would help him get elected to Congress. Ferguson also promised to help place a normal school and an agricultural school in East Texas, wherever Fuller wanted. (Fuller lived in East Texas.) Fuller flatly refused to go along with Ferguson, and it was then that he decided to have the governor impeached.

That afternoon the board met, sitting in executive session at the suggestion of the governor, and each man expressed his views. Only Governor Ferguson and Mr. Doughty favored Abilene; the others were divided.

After the discussion, Fuller and the board's secretary, Mr. Thompson, prepared the ballots, and the first vote was taken. The results were two for Abilene, and one each for San Angelo, Haskell and Snyder. On the orders of the governor, the first ballots were destroyed, and a second vote was taken.

When the ballots were taken up, Lieutenant Governor Hobby read the results. He first announced that Abilene had two votes, but Governor Ferguson corrected him, saying no, Abilene had three votes, Hobby agreed. Afterwards, they made the selection unanimous by a voice vote.

Fuller now insisted to the House of Representatives that he had never voted for Abilene, and never told anyone that he had voted for Abilene. He looked directly at Jim Ferguson as he made the statement, and newsmen would report that he looked the governor straight in the eye, recalling Ferguson's challenge in his Walnut Springs speech.

Fuller continued that he had at first declined to make public how he had voted; Davis and Hobby had acted first, both announcing that they had not voted for Abilene. Fuller had then written to Hobby and Davis and wired Ferguson that the board should be reconvened.

Instead, Fuller met with Governor Ferguson on July 6, and at that meeting, Ferguson refused to reconvene the board. Ferguson also suggested that a statement should be issued so that the matter could be settled. The statement said that the selection of Abilene had been fair and accurate.

Fuller told the governor to call in the other members, including Lieutenant Governor Hobby, and it was at that point, Fuller claimed, that the governor tricked him. Hobby couldn't come to Austin, said Ferguson, but he was in favor of the statement. Reluctantly, Fuller signed it.

After the meeting, Ferguson told Fuller that he was going to send him to Congress and mentioned that he knew that Fuller was trying to impeach him. He broached the subject of a loan, saying that he had plenty of money.

"When he mentioned giving me a check," declared the speaker of the House, "I saw a chance to catch him, and accepted." He said that Governor Ferguson gave him a check for $400 and $100 in cash, and in return Fuller gave the governor his personal note for $500.

W. A. Hanger cross-examined the speaker briefly on Monday and again, in more depth, on Tuesday. It is fair to say that Hanger made a shambles of Fuller's credibility as a witness.

Fuller denied to Hanger that he had ever told Representative McFarland that he had stood by the governor. He denied ever hearing Ferguson tell Dr. Cooper of Abilene, "That was the third vote," pointing to Fuller as he said it.

Why had Fuller later signed the statement that the selection of Abilene had been fair? Because Ferguson had misled him, had told him that Lieutenant Governor Hobby favored the statement. Did Fuller think the vote had been fair? No, something had been "put over."

Hanger: "If you knew all this and also had decided to impeach the governor many days before, why did you sign the statement saying the selection was on the square?"

Fuller: "For the reasons I have stated. I was misled."

Hanger: Regarding Fuller's statement that Ferguson had promised to locate a normal school in East Texas, wasn't it a fact that Fuller had once written to the governor, asking his help in obtaining a college for that area? Yes, Fuller admitted that it was true. And hadn't the governor expressly told Fuller that he wouldn't make any deals on the schools? No, said Fuller.

Hanger read a letter that Fuller had written to Ferguson, asking that the East Texas Normal School be fairly located; then another letter asking that Ferguson consider Fuller's son for an appointment.

Hanger then asked Fuller if he had needed money on the day he took the loan from Ferguson. No, not really. Wasn't it true that at the time, he owed $1,500 to a man named Churchill, who was pressing him for the money? No, said Fuller, and he wanted to explain that. "In proper time," said Hanger.

Wasn't it true that in May 1915, Fuller had made a contract with Churchill, a Fort Worth contractor, by which Churchill had given Fuller $3,000 for his help in obtaining the contract to rebuild the San Jacinto County Courthouse in Cold Springs? (Cold Springs was Fuller's home.) No, insisted Fuller.

He said that he didn't remember any contract, but he had taken $2,500 from Churchill in a pre-arranged plan to keep grafters out of any deal to build a new courthouse. The contract had not been awarded to Churchill, and Fuller had later returned the money — or at least $2,250 of it. He had kept possession of the money the entire time.

No, he had never written to Churchill that Churchill would have to wait for the money until Fuller could collect it from others.

The whole thing had been a pre-arranged plan. Fuller had caught a bunch of Fort Worth contractors redhanded, trying to buy the contract to build the San Jacinto County Courthouse. He had received the $2,500 as an attorney's fee — that was Churchill's name for it. Besides, Hanger himself had known of the deal. Fuller had been impressed with Churchill's statement that Hanger was interested in the deal.

Hanger: "Did you think I was a grafter when you asked me to assist you to the speakership and when you sought appointment as judge in the Beaumont district?"

Fuller sputtered. He had gained an impression at the time of the deal, he said. He had not sought the Beaumont judgeship; Governor Ferguson had offered it to him. Later he had determined that the offer was insincere and had decided to work for the appointment himself.

"Didn't Churchill try to collect the $250 still due and another note for $700 from you?"

"He tried to blackmail me several times."

Did Fuller remember writing a letter praising Churchill? No. After he had paid back $1,500 of the money, did Fuller write to Churchill and ask him to come down some? No. Had Fuller ever brought a grafter before a Grand Jury? No. Had he ever solicited a $500 payment from Churchill. No.

Hanger then read a letter that Fuller had written to Thomas J. West, a judge in Fort Worth who occupied an office next to Churchill's. "We need $500," said the letter, "on the proposition we are advancing."

Fuller said that he had never met Judge West; he did not remember any such letter. Did he recognize his own signature? Yes, Fuller admitted that his signature was on the letter.

"You got a $500 check in reply, didn't you?" asked Hanger, and he produced a check. Fuller admitted that he had received it.

Hanger read a document signed by Fuller which said that if Churchill got the contract to rebuild the San Jacinto County Courthouse, all money that Fuller had received from Churchill would remain Fuller's permanently. And he read a letter Fuller had written to Churchill, telling the contractor that his credentials were entirely satisfactory.

By the time Hanger was finished with Fuller, it was evident that there was a serious question about the integrity of the man who had brought the charges against Governor Ferguson and called for the special session to impeach him.

Responding to Chester Terrell on redirect questioning, Fuller lamely repeated that he had only been trying to catch the grafters. When Churchill offered him the money, Fuller immediately informed the county judge, whom he had known for fifteen years.

Did Fuller believe that Ferguson had written the "all fair" statement about the new college? Yes, Fuller did.

The next day, Wednesday the 15th, Crane brought Texas Adjutant General Hutchins to the stand and asked him about the governor's bodyguards. Hutchins testified that he had kept a Texas Ranger stationed at the Governor's Mansion since May 15 to look after the governor. Ferguson had received threatening letters, and Hutchins was afraid that the governor's life might be in danger.

He believed that two Rangers should be stationed in the gallery of the House now, but he had stopped posting them there after Speaker Fuller had objected to them.

How many Rangers did Hutchins have on duty in Travis County at the present time? Six, said the Adjutant General — two captains, two sergeants, and two enlisted men. At what cost to the State? Hutchins guessed that the cost was about $600 a year. Was Governor Ferguson the only governor to ever have Rangers for bodyguards? Hutchins wasn't certain about that; he thought other governors had used Rangers as bodyguards on trips. Crane wasn't talking about trips; he meant here, in Austin. Hutchins wasn't sure. He pointed out that Ferguson hadn't requested the guard and had accepted it only on Hutchins' recommendation.

On cross-examination, Hanger asked if the six Rangers in Austin were used for other missions, and Hutchins replied that they were sent throughout the state. Chester Terrell interjected that there certainly seemed to be more than six Rangers in Austin. Hutchins admitted that there were more than six Texas Rangers in town, but only six of them were stationed on duty there.

On Thursday, Jim Ferguson sent a governor's message to the legislature. The drought in West Texas had reached terrible proportions, said the message, and conditions were severe. It was the worst drought in thirty years, and he wanted to prevent suffering due to lack of food or clothes. Having recently toured the western counties, he knew that the situation was not being exaggerated, and he called on the legislature to give prompt consideration to providing relief for the people in West Texas. On the same day, in the House chamber, W. A. Hanger began the defense of Jim Ferguson.

Hanger began by calling the man who had served as secretary to the locating board, W. E. Thommason. Thommason testified that he had been planning on moving west, and so was glad to get the opportunity to tour the western counties with the board. The job paid $10 a day, plus expenses.

Hanger asked Thommason about the crucial vote, when Jim Ferguson was accused of "putting one over." Thommason answered that when the vote was taken, Speaker Fuller was sitting six or seven feet away from the governor. On the second ballot, the vote was three for Abilene, one for Snyder, and one for Amarillo.

Thommason was certain that the vote was absolutely correct. He had been surprised when Abilene won and had examined the ballots carefully. Governor Ferguson never touched the ballots after they had been passed out.

Chester Terrell tried to attack Thommason's testimony. Wasn't it true, he asked, that Speaker Fuller had told Thommason that the governor was trying to place the school in Abilene, but that Fuller opposed it? Yes, that was true, said Thommason.

Wasn't it true that the governor had been the first to suggest that the meeting be held in executive session? No, Thommason didn't agree with that. The governor hadn't made a suggestion; he had merely asked if the session should be executive and had said that he would be governed by the board. There had been some discussion, and they had all decided to meet in executive session.

Next, Hanger called Representative M. M. McFarland, who testified that on June 29, he wired Fuller to stand by the gover-

nor, and on July 25, Fuller told him that he had stood by Ferguson. On cross-examination, however, McFarland admitted that
when he wired Fuller to stand by the governor, he had thought
Ferguson favored San Angelo.

Hanger called Dr. O. H. Cooper of Abilene, a former representative and former president of Baylor University, who told
of a meeting he had had with Governor Ferguson in Austin.
During the meeting, Speaker Fuller had come in, and Ferguson
had said, ''He's your third vote,'' pointing to Fuller as he said
it. Fuller had been very gracious and had not contradicted the
governor.

Hanger then brought to the stand Miss Mattie McCracken,
a long-distance telephone operator from Abilene. Miss Mc-
Cracken said that she had heard Speaker Fuller talk over the
phone to an Abilene newsman, and had heard Fuller tell the reporter that he had voted for Abilene.

On cross-examination, though, she admitted that she knew
that two hours after the phone call, the Abilene reporter had
telegraphed Fuller that he had not been able to hear on the
phone and he wanted confirmation by telegraph. Fuller had
not given the confirmation.

And finally, State Representative Debogory testified for
Hanger that when the board had visited Abilene, Fuller told
him that Abilene was certain to get the new college, based on
the showing that Abilene had made.

On Friday, August 17, Hanger called a deputy U.S. mar-
shall from Galveston, who testified that he had once been a special man for the Texas Rangers in Austin. The deputy said that a
Ranger had once served as a bodyguard for Governor Will Hogg
during the 1890s. The Ranger had been posted after Governor
Hogg had received threatening letters, and the deputy didn't
think that the governor had even been aware that the Ranger
was guarding him.

Hanger then called Wilbur P. Allen, the chairman of the
University of Texas Board of Regents, and asked him to explain
the $5,000 bail bond that Governor Ferguson had remanded to
him. Allen said that the bond had been posted by himself and

some others for one Louis Rodriguez, who had worked on a ranch owned by Allen's brother, and who was also accused of murder. Rodriguez had later jumped bail and fled to Mexico, and there was still a $1,000 reward out for him. Allen claimed that the remanding of the bond had nothing to do with any action he had taken with reference to the University of Texas.

Under cross-examination, Allen denied that he had ever tried to pressure President Vinson or Secretary Lomax into resigning. He supported President Vinson. Prosecutor Crane was skeptical. Wasn't it a fact that Allen was doing all he could to help Governor Ferguson, and would have even resigned to help the governor? Allen replied that he would do anything he could to help the university.

In answer to a question, Allen said that he did not believe that university professors should have lifetime jobs, but instead should be kept only for good cause. On the question of fraternities, he disagreed with the governor; Allen himself had been a member of a fraternity and had held national office in it. No, he had not voted to fire Dr. Coffer, but he would have if Governor Ferguson had asked him to.

Wasn't it true, asked Crane, that the regents were planning to fire Dr. Vinson in October? No, said Allen. What were the board's plans for the position of president of the university?

They would like to get Dr. Stockton Axton, President Woodrow Wilson's brother-in-law, answered Allen. If they could get Axton, Allen would vote for him.

Hadn't the four university professors been fired even though a legislative committee had determined that they were not guilty of any wrongdoing? Yes, admitted Allen.

In the afternoon of August 17, Hanger called his chief defense witness, the governor of Texas, James Edward Ferguson.

In taking the witness stand in his own impeachment proceedings, Jim Ferguson was in a sense setting a constitutional precedent. Under the old English Parliamentary system, officers who were being impeached did not appear either before the House of Commons or the House of Lords. The U.S. system of government was, of course, based largely on the English system, and the Texas system was based on both the U.S. and the English models.

When M. M. Crane called Jim Ferguson to the stand at the outset of the proceedings, Ferguson counsel insisted that he had the right to not testify until he had heard the evidence against him. In all probability, Hanger could just as easily have argued that Jim Ferguson was not required to testify at all; indeed he did not even have to be present at impeachment proceedings against him. When the U.S. Congress impeached President Andrew Johnson, the president did not attend either the proceedings of the House or his trial before the U.S. Senate.

Indeed, it could have been argued that Governor Ferguson did not have the right or the privilege to testify before the Texas Legislature at all. But the legislature did not consider that argument, and the counsel for the House, Mr. Crane, was anxious to have the chance to question Governor Ferguson. By taking the stand to testify in his own behalf, Ferguson was assuring Crane of the chance to cross-examine him; and he was also forfeiting his right to later decline to testify if Crane should call him again.

As he took the stand on the 17th, Ferguson began a point-by-point rebuttal of each of the charges Speaker Fuller had brought against him. W. A. Hanger questioned him and prompted him, reading the charges, eliciting Ferguson's view of the circumstances of each. Today they covered the first six charges; Ferguson would return to the stand tomorrow.

Hanger read the first charge, that Ferguson had failed to refund to the State the money that he had used to buy groceries and gasoline and other items instead of fuel and lights for the Governor's Mansion.

Ferguson: The original suit had concerned his predecessor, Governor Colquitt. At the March investigation, he had said that he would return any amounts for which the courts said he was liable; but Judge Calhoun had ruled that certain accounts were liable and others were not, and had not said which purchases were not allowed.

Nevertheless, Ferguson had investigated on his own and had taken up deficiency warrants for $2,059, covering the various expenditures that had been complained about. (Taking up a

W. A. HANGER, a celebrated trial lawyer from Fort Worth, served as Jim Ferguson's chief defense counsel before the Texas House of Representatives as well as the High Court of Impeachment. Hanger was a former state senator and a political leader in Tarrant County. A graduate of the then-famous Cumberland Law School in Lebanon, Tennessee, he had a wide reputation as a shrewd defense attorney.

— *Photo Courtesy of Mrs. Earl Wilson*

deficiency warrant is similar to the modern practice of signing a note payable.)

The legislature had made no provision for labor at the Governor's Mansion, said Ferguson, so he had paid for such labor out of his own pocket.

Hanger read Judge Calhoun's opinion and also a list of deficiency warrants that Ferguson had taken up for groceries. Then Hanger read Fuller's second charge — that Ferguson had taken the Canyon City Normal College fire insurance funds out of a bank where they were drawing interest and placed them in the Temple State Bank.

Ferguson: Yes, it was true that he had received the money. A few days after he became governor, the legislature appropriated the insurance settlement, plus an additional $50,000 to rebuild the college. He did not then nor now understand that the money had to be kept in the state treasury; it was a separate fund. He had kept in the Temple Sate Bank only so that it would be handy and could be used for the purpose for which it had been appropriated. While Colquitt was in office, he could deposit the money for interest, but Ferguson had to keep the money handy. Every cent he had received from Governor Colquitt had been used to rebuild the college.

Hanger read the third charge, that on August 23, 1915, Ferguson had used $5,600 of the state's funds in the Temple State Bank to pay a personal obligation.

Ferguson: He had several accounts in the Temple State Bank — a personal account, a special account, an account for his ranch, and his governor's account.

His personal secretary, J. H. Davis, and the man who was then the cashier at the Temple State Bank, C. A. Hughes, looked after all his personal affairs. They took care of his business dealings and paid his bills. They had never told him about the $5,600 payment. The first he had heard about it had been when he had testified before the Travis County Grand Jury.

"That it should have been charged to the governor's account was a mistake of which I knew nothing until long after. It could as well have been charged to my special account, which had over $16,000 in it, or it could have been brought to my attention, and I could have fixed it.''

Hanger asked Ferguson to explain his special account, and Ferguson said that the account had originated in litigation over timberland in Liberty County. Ferguson had sold the land for $48,000. Pending the outcome of the litigation, it had been agreed that the Dayton Lumber Company would pay $2,000 a month into a special account for each month that it cut timber on the land. On the date in question, three-fourths of the money in the account was Ferguson's.

Hanger read the fourth charge — that Ferguson had profited from the deposit of over $100,000 of state funds in the Temple State Bank.

Ferguson: ''I suppose this refers to the secretary of state's account. I told the secretary of state I would appreciate it if he would put some of the franchise taxes money in the Temple State Bank, and franky I wanted these deposits as large as possible. There was no interest to be gained, and the treasury would not receive until the end of the quarter. It was the custom to keep the money in somebody's bank, and by way of making a showing, I was willing to have some of the money put into the Temple State Bank.''

Hanger mentioned the deposit of $250,000 in the American National Bank of Austin to the credit of the secretary of state's account in the Temple State Bank.

Ferguson: ''The secretary of state made out five drafts of $50,000 each to T. H. Heard of the Temple Bank. Mr. Heard wanted to meet the officers of the American National Bank, and I took him down and introduced him. That is how I happened to be present when the $250,000 was deposited. Few state accounts are of any renumerative value. The best that I know of is the university account.''

He read a list of balances that the University of Texas had maintained in the American National Bank over a three-year period. Then he shouted:

''If I ought to be impeached for keeping the secretary of state's account in the Temple State Bank for three months, then

I say the Board of Regents ought to be hanged for keeping the university account in the American National Bank three years!''

This pronouncement caused an outburst in the gallery, and it took a few moments for the commotion to die down. After it did, Hanger read the fifth charge — that Ferguson had induced the Temple State Bank to lend him $170,000, which was more than the bank's entire capital and surplus.

Ferguson answered that during this year he had decided to clear up his indebtedness to the Temple State Bank and had done so. He had been unable to obtain credit at other banks but had appealed to friends, who had raised $156,000 and placed it at his disposal. He was no longer in debt to the Temple State Bank.

Ferguson no doubt believed that this response would satisfy the House and would negate the charge that he had induced the official's of his old bank to lend him too much money. But the reply that he gave would actually cause him much more trouble; for M. M. Crane and the House of Representatives would later want to know who Ferguson's friends were and why they had loaned him such a large sum of money. Ferguson and Hanger did not realize their blunder.

The next day, Saturday, August 18, they continued with the rebuttal of the charges. Hanger reminded the governor that he was charged with vetoing the appropriation for the University of Texas, which in effect violated the constitutional provision for the maintenance of the university.

Ferguson read Governor Culberson's 1895 veto of certain items in the appropriation for the University of Texas. Then the constitutional provision that the university be limited in its use of funds to ''the maintenance of a university of the first class.''

He hadn't violated the constitution, said Ferguson. He had vetoed the appropriation because he thought the permanent fund of the university was not being properly used; and also because it was extravagant; and also the faculty had formed a mob that had tried to browbeat him into signing the bill.

The governor launched into an attack on the university.

The ratio of students to employees was eight to one. In two years, he had appropriated $1.2 million to the university; while in all the thirty-three previous years, only $4.4 million had been appropriated for it. More than one hundred counties sent only one student to the university, and fifty-three counties didn't send a student at all. The cost of educating students at the university was $308 each.

Still, the governor said, if the House passed by a two-thirds vote the appropriation bill that had recently passed in the Senate, he would let it become law without his signature. He didn't mention the fact, but of course a two-thirds majority would have indicated that the House would override him if he chose to veto the appropriation. This didn't mean, he said, that he was receding from his original position. He just felt that no good would come of yet another session of the legislature, even though he still felt that the appropriation would be extravagant.

Ferguson claimed that "criticism had been heaped upon him" because he had inquired into the management of the university; yet, the constitution, he said, gave him the power to inquire into the management of every institution of the state. It gave him the right — if cause was shown — to remove the officials of any institution.

He went on that his charge of corruption at the university was substantiated by the fact that professors had bought mileage books for $25 and charged them to the state at $30. And by the fact that Dr. Caswell Ellis, who was in charge of extension work, had drawn a salary of $3,250 from the university and another $1,193 from the San Antonio School Board.

He read a statement that Dr. Vinson had made to a group of students, saying that the university no longer had to "bow down and beg but could instead demand what it needed."

Then he read an article from the student newspaper at the university, *The Daily Texan,* which reported that some voters in the fourth ward — which included the university community — had scratched Ferguson's name off the ballot and written-in P. Lender, a black man. Ferguson was indignant. This, he said, showed their disrespectful attitude toward him.

He sent on to describe his relationship with President Vin-

University of Texas student protest march against Governor Jim Ferguson, May 28, 1917. The students marched to the capitol and held a rally outside the governor's office, breaking up a meeting of the Board of Regents. This infuriated Ferguson, who soon thereafter vetoed the appropriation for the university. Ferguson was so angry that he had to be kept from going out to fight some of the students. He always referred to students in this photo as a "mob."

— *Photo from Baker Texas History Center,*
University of Texas, Austin

son. When they first met, said Ferguson, Vinson had asked him for his cooperation and had asked him to speak frankly. Ferguson obviously did:

> I thanked the doctor and told him that if he wanted me to speak frankly, I would. I told him then candidly that I thought it would be a mistake for him to enter on his work with the thought that he had been selected for the place because he was thought capable of filling it.
>
> He expressed surprise, and I explained that we had been searching for a president for 18 months, and in all that time not a single man had thought of him as being capable of filling the job, although they had seen him every morning before breakfast.
>
> I have never thought Dr. Vinson could fill the place. There are at least 20 men at the university of higher educational attainment than he. He did not make a success at his former job. I told him that he had been given the presidency to be a figurehead for those who had appointed him, and I hoped he'd show himself big enough to run the school himself. I asked him if he had any plan for running the university, and he said he was not yet in office and had none.

Ferguson said that he told Vinson that four men — Battle, Mayes, Potts, and Lomax — should be discharged.

Then he turned to the question of fraternities at the university, and over objections was allowed to read a pamphlet that had been prepared by non-fraternity students. The pamphlet complained that fraternities were clubs for rich men's sons, were snobbish, and generated class distinctions. The non-fraternity students said that they were called "barbarians" and felt themselves to be "underdogs." The pamphlet called on the Board of Regents to help eliminate the fraternities.

Hanger prompted Ferguson to discuss the charge that he had removed members of the university Board of Regents without good cause.

Ferguson replied that he had not removed any regent except Dr. Jones, who had moved to Virginia and had not been attending meetings. He said that it had become evident that Will Hogg and Will Harrell were trying to defy him and elect a university president who would do their wishes. And so, since Jones was out of the state, Ferguson had appointed a replacement.

Then, during the Galveston meeting of the regents, Dr. McReynolds had left to go to Dallas to attend to a sick relative. Ferguson called McReynolds and told him that he was badly needed at the meeting, and McReynolds then offered to resign. Ferguson had approved of the idea, and McReynolds telegramed his resignation. Ferguson appointed W. G. Love to replace him.

He added that two other regents — Rabbi Faber and J. W. Butler — had resigned of their own accord.

Hanger asked Ferguson if he had told Dr. Brents, during the meeting that the student demonstration broke up, that the regents would have to fire President Vinson or Ferguson would veto the university appropriation. No, said Ferguson. He had merely called the regents' attention to the need for a competent man to head the university.

"I asked Brents what he was going to do about that mob, what he was going to do about it. I asked what he would do if he found that Dr. Vinson was in any way responsible for the demonstration. He replied, 'I am not in favor of doing anything to Dr. Vinson.' I told him that I thought the time had come when something should be done.

"If a mob was gathering to deride the governor, I wanted to know if he was going to stand with me or against me, as he was my apointee. I told him if Vinson and the faculty let such a thing be pulled off, they should be kicked out, root and branch."

Hanger directed Ferguson to the matter of the West Texas A. and M. locating board.

Ferguson testified that prior to the trip he approved the appointment of W. E. Thommason as secretary to the board. The other members had already announced that they favored Thommason, and during the trip, he proved to be of great assistance. Lieutenant Governor Hobby had been unable to make the trip, but had promised to come to Austin for the voting to select a site for the new college. The board embarked on June 6, and after touring the western cities, disbandoned at Amarillo, agreeing to return to Austin for the voting.

Back in Austin, Ferguson met informally with the other members, and since the lieutenant governor needed time to inform himself on the matter, they agreed to hold the meeting on June 29. Ferguson claimed that he told Hobby that he believed Abilene should get the new school, because it was the best city in that part of the state and the center of the population there. Hobby answered that he would leave the matter in the governor's hands.

About an hour before the meeting, said Ferguson, Speaker Fuller came in. Fuller was very excited and talked about his friends not understanding that the school couldn't go to more than one town. Ferguson told the speaker to "get it out of his head" that the school could be located in two cities.

Ferguson testified that he told Fuller that he would make a great mistake if he considered only the claims of his friends; he should vote for Abilene because it was the best town. Fuller replied that he was obligated to Bruce Bryant of Haskell, who already had two votes committed to that city. He said that he was going to vote for Haskell on the first ballot, but if the other two votes didn't show up, he would then vote with the governor for Abilene.

It was Fuller who suggested that the meeting should be held in executive session; it was Fuller who wanted to "get together and lock the door."

Ferguson himself cut the ballots. On the first vote, he saw Lieutenant Governor Hobby write "San Angelo" on his ballot and saw Fuller write "Haskell" on his. He couldn't help but see their ballots; they were only eight feet away. Later he saw Fuller's second ballot when the speaker dropped it into the hat, and he saw that "Abilene" was written on it.

Ferguson later told Fuller, "You voted for Abilene, you know you did, and you ought to come out like a man and say that you did." And the speaker, Ferguson claimed, answered: "I know I voted for Abilene, as I promised you I would, but don't force me to say that. It would ruin me.'' And Ferguson told the speaker of the House that ''he was ruined already.''

Hanger mentioned the matter of the post of labor commissioner, and the fact that Ferguson was allegedly allowing a man who had been refused confirmation by the Texas Senate to continue to serve in the post.

Ferguson testified that he had sent C. W. Woodman's name to the Senate as his nominee for labor commissioner, but the Senate had declined to confirm him. Ferguson later sent the name of Frank Swor, who was indeed confirmed by the Senate, although Swor had failed to qualify. Swor had not refused to qualify; he had simply failed to do so. Ferguson did not know why; it was not because of any suggestion that he had made. He understood that Swor would qualify either today or tomorrow. Woodman had continued to draw the salary of labor commissioner, but that would stop as soon as Swor qualified.

Ferguson returned to the witness stand on Monday, August 20, as the third full week of the House proceedings began. He and his counsel Hanger opened with a response to Fuller's allegation concerning Ferguson's remanding of a bail bond to the chairman of the University of Texas Board of Regents.

The governor explained that Wilbur P. Allen had told him that he believed he could bring the accused criminal, Rodriguez, back from Mexico. To allow a forfeiture of the bond would have caused hardship for the others who were in on it, and besides, Ferguson never enforced a bond if local authorities didn't wish it done.

''I concluded finally to remit the bond,'' he said, ''as to enforce it would neither bring the man Rodriguez killed back to life nor Rodriguez back to trial.'' The matter had had no effect on any of his offical acts as governor.

Hanger asked if Ferguson had ever attempted to coerce any of the regents, or members of any other board. No, said Ferguson, he had never coerced anyone; although he had ''never failed to appeal to the reason of those concerned, with all the power that God had given him.''

Hanger mentioned Ferguson's letter to the Texas Supreme Court, calling the justices' attention to the constitutional provision for the allocation of funds for expenses at the governor's mansion. Ferguson responded that he was simply trying to "make record" in the matter and had no intention of trying to influence anyone.

Regarding his letter to the Beaumont Court of Appeals, he explained for Hanger that he considered the court's decision on the Dayton Lumber case a terrible judicial blunder. He had nothing to hide, he added.

He testified for Hanger that he had never tried to influence Speaker Fuller. As he started to speak, Ferguson turned around and addressed the speaker of the House, asking Fuller to come around in front, where Ferguson could look at him. Fuller left his seat and stepped around to take a chair in front of the governor. Then, looking at Fuller, Ferguson continued his testimony.

Ferguson said that he had asked Speaker Fuller how his campaign for Congress was coming along, and the speaker answered, "fine," except that he needed money. Fuller said that he in fact needed $500. Ferguson started to give Fuller a check for $500, but Fuller pleaded that he needed some cash. The two men drew up a note, Ferguson said, and he then gave Fuller $100 in cash and a check for $400. Fuller said that he wouldn't be able to repay the loan very soon, and Ferguson told him that was alright. During the conversation, they did not discuss the matter of the new college, and nothing was said about the written statement that Abilene had been chosen fairly and accurately.

The difference between Ferguson's account of his loan to Fuller and the speaker's version was so great that the House of Representatives was obviously going to have to decide which of the two men were lying.

Hanger asked Ferguson about the Texas Rangers who had guarded him, and Ferguson replied that these were dangerous times. There had been threats against his life. When he had authorized a $1,000 reward for the raider De la Rosa, the outlaw had responded by putting out a $1,000 reward for Ferguson's head.

Ferguson read a letter he had received from a judge, warning him that an unnamed person was going to try to kill him; and another letter from a man who said he would kill Ferguson if he vetoed the university appropriation. If he vetoed the appropriation, said the letter, he would "wake up in hell inside of three months."

Now, Hanger surrendered his chief defense witness. Jim Ferguson had given his version of reality to the House of Representatives, but now he would have to face M. M. Crane. Two weeks after he had first called Jim Ferguson to the stand, Crane would finally have the chance to question the governor of Texas. From Ferguson's standpoint, the results would be devastating.

Crane: Had the governor paid back the $2,000 light and fuel fund since the March hearings?

Ferguson: He never understood that anyone wanted him to pay that money back. If the legislature wanted him to pay it back, he would do so.

Crane read Ferguson's testimony before the investigating committee, in which Ferguson promised to repay the money if the Texas Supreme Court refused to reopen the case.

Crane: Didn't Ferguson know that Judge Fly had ruled that he couldn't use money from the appropriation to buy groceries?

Ferguson: He knew of the decision.

Crane: Alright, had he made any effort to reimburse the state?

Ferguson: Not at all. He didn't understand the matter in that way.

Crane: As governor, did he consider it good policy to ignore a decision of the Supreme Court, pending a motion for rehearing?

Ferguson: That would depend on the circumstances. Judge Calhoun had differed from Judge Fly. He had engaged counsel to carry the matter to the Supreme Court.

Crane: Wasn't it true that the action to obtain a writ of error was more in the interest of the man who happened to be governor, than in the interest of the people of Texas?

Ferguson: He didn't know. There was an injustice in

holding the governor's salary to $4,000 a year; it should have been rectified.

Crane: Wasn't it true that every court in the state was against Ferguson?

Ferguson: The legislature was against the courts too. As soon as the legislature said it wanted the money, he would give them his check.

Crane asked about the Canyon City Normal fire insurance settlement. Ferguson admitted that he had put $40,000 of the money in the Temple State Bank, and another $5,000 in a bank in Heidenheimer (a small town near Temple), in which he was also a stockholder. The money in those two banks had not drawn interest.

Wasn't it true that the governor never cashed checks on the $40,000 at all, but instead all checks were drawn on the American National Bank in Austin?

Yes.

Why was that?

The contractors came to Austin for settlement, Ferguson explained. He would give checks to the state treasurer, who would then ask the Temple State Bank to remit the money to the American National.

Crane: Hadn't Ferguson taken the insurance settlement funds from banks where they were drawing interest and not given them to the state treasurer so that he could put them in banks where they could draw more interest?

Ferguson: Yes.

Crane: "Do you recall that you had over $300,000 of state funds in the Temple State Bank, but only $50,000 in cash?"

"But you must remember that we had cash in other banks."

"Then it was of some value to you to have the state's money in the Temple bank?"

Ferguson first said yes, but then challenged the point. Any bank would be stupid to laon out state funds knowing they were subject to quarterly recall. The state funds had just helped the Temple bank "make a showing."

Crane questioned Ferguson about his special account in the Temple State Bank, and the governor made some new admissions.

The account had been opened as a result of litigation with the Dayton Lumber Company, and the funds were required to remain in the account until the litigation was settled. Ferguson couldn't draw on the account until the settlement was reached, late in 1916.

Crane: The $5,600 which the governor had paid on August 23, 1915, could not have been paid from the special account as Ferguson had claimed, could it?

Ferguson answered that three-fourths of the money in the account was his.

Crane's questioning continued into the afternoon session. Did the governor recall that the word *groceries* had been stricken from the 1915 mansion appropriation bill? Ferguson did not.

Wasn't it a fact that Ferguson's account and the account of the Bell-Bosque Ranch had been greatly overdrawn in 1915 and 1916? Yes. And that his total indebtedness was about $155,000? Yes.

Hadn't he practically guaranteed the notes of J. H. Davis and A. F. Ferguson, with which he had cleared up his affairs? Yes. And he had borrowed all that money knowing that the banking laws prohibited it?

Yes, admitted Ferguson, but he had paid it all back. Besides, he said, a certain bank in which Crane himself was interested had violated the banking laws and committed prejury in its statements.

Crane: "That is denied! You can't get away with that stuff, Governor. Just answer my questions."

Ferguson: "Well, if the banking laws were enforced, every banker in the state would go to the penitentiary."

Crane asked if Ferguson hadn't prosecuted an Amarillo banker for the same practices he himself had followed. Ferguson admitted that he had, but still insisted that he had not violated the spirit of the law.

Crane: Was it not a fact that Ferguson had withdrawn practically all the deposits in the special account before the Dayton Lumber case had been settled?

Ferguson: Well, four-fifths of that money was his, apparently increasing his share.

Crane: Hadn't Ferguson been sued by one of the litigants in the case for an accounting in the matter?

Ferguson: There had been an attempt to blackmail him.

Crane read the portion of the penal code that called for a penitentiary sentence for the misapplication of public funds. He asked if Ferguson had been familiar with the law that prohibited the deposit of more than $50,000 of state funds in any one bank when he allowed $250,000 to be deposited in the American National Bank to the credit of the Temple State Bank.

Yes, Ferguson answered that he was familiar with the law, but he had not violated *any* law. He had not received the money as a repository, and he wasn't required to put the money in the state treasury until a certain later date.

Crane returned to the matter of the $5,600 that Ferguson had used to repay a personal bank note. How soon would the $5,600 be repaid to the state?

The records would show, answered Ferguson.

Did Ferguson believe that the law meant that a state official could use state funds like that?

That had been an error, Ferguson insisted. The state had lost no money.

Why had Ferguson deposited the Canyon Normal insurance money in the Temple State Bank?

"I wanted to protect the people from those contractors."

"Couldn't the money be protected if it was in the state treasury? Couldn't you hold the state treasurer responsible?"

"I couldn't hold the state treasurer responsible for anything. Sam Sparks controls him."

Crane mentioned that Ferguson had personally taken $60,000 to the Temple State Bank in February and deposited it. Hadn't he tried to use that $60,000 to show the directors of the bank that he was more valuable to them than anyone else?

No, not at all.

Crane returned to the matter of the $5,600. Ferguson replied that he had first heard of the matter when he testified before the Travis County Grand Jury.

What had he told the Grand Jury?

He had told them that he knew nothing about the charge or what it was for.

Then Crane asked Ferguson a question that would have a profound outcome on the impeachment proceedings; he asked him a question about a subject that Ferguson himself had introduced into the proceedings. He asked the governor who had loaned him the money with which he had cleared up his bank debts.

Ferguson: "I'll be frank with you. I got that money when I was facing bankruptcy. I promised not to tell who gave me the money. I cannot disclose those names."

Neither Ferguson nor Crane nor Hanger understood the impact that Ferguson's answer would have on the outcome of the impeachment proceedings, and for the moment, Crane only pressed the matter lightly.

Had the money been given to Ferguson in currency?

Yes.

Why wasn't it paid to him in check?

The loaners didn't want their names associated with Ferguson's affairs.

Again, who had loaned him the money and when?

The money had been loaned to Ferguson in April. He couldn't tell by whom. No one looking for a school had given him the money; but he must decline positively to let the public into that phase of his private affairs. Crane went on to another matter.

Hadn't Ferguson told the Board of Regents that if they didn't fire certain professors at the university he would fire the regents?

No, he had told them that if they didn't clear things up out there, he would have to exercise his constitutional rights to get someone who would.

Didn't the governor think it unfair to discharge men without a hearing and blacken their futures by not stating the reasons for firing them?

That depended, said Ferguson. Vinson and the regents had fired Professor Keasby by telegram. (Keasby was a friend of Ferguson.)

But wasn't there a reason for that? Hadn't Keasby expressed himself in a way inimical to the government? (Keasby had given a speech opposing war with Germany.)

Ferguson replied that he guessed there were others as bad as Keasby.

Crane asked about Ferguson's statement that he didn't think Vinson was qualified to be president of the University of Texas. No, said the governor, he didn't believe that a graduate of Austin College (a small college in Sherman, Texas) was capable of heading the university.

If the appropriation bill was passed, wasn't Ferguson going to insist that Vinson be fired? No, Ferguson wasn't going to insist on anything.

What had he done to Major Littlefield? Hadn't he taken $250,000 out of the American National Bank on the day that Littlefield voted to keep Dr. Vinson? (The American National was Littlefield's bank.) No, the money had been taken out before then.

Didn't Ferguson think he had been discourteous to Dr. Vinson by telling him that he hadn't been chosen for his ability? No.

What was the difference between professors charging full fare for mileage books and Ferguson using the mansion appropriation to buy groceries?

His statements, said Ferguson, showed facts.

But his statements showed groceries listed as incidentals, didn't they? Ferguson admitted that they did.

Did Ferguson intend to continue to remove regents who did not do his bidding?

He wouldn't shirk his constitutional duty, if those men weren't doing all that they should, said the governor.

Hadn't he appointed Kelley, Mathews, Brent, and Love so that they could fire Dr. Vinson? No, but if a better man could be found, Ferguson was all for it.

Whom did he have in mind — Superintendent Doughty or Dr. Axton, Woodrow Wilson's brother-in-law? Yes, Ferguson liked the idea of Dr. Axton.

That evening, with Ferguson due to return to the stand

tomorrow, the papers headlined his refusal to reveal who had loaned him the $156,000.

Tuesday, August 21 — Crane hammered at Ferguson with a barrage of questions on the university matter and also Ferguson's finances. Finally he came to the matter that everyone was waiting for.

How would it hurt Ferguson's friends if he made their names public?

They were probably influenced by business decisions, said Ferguson, and didn't want to get mixed up in a political wrangel. The public had no right to inquire into his personal business, so long as he performed his official duties faithfully. Nobody who belonged to a special class that had any interest in legislation had loaned him the money.

"I refuse absolutely to give you any information on this point. If it costs me my office and plunges me into bankruptcy, I must still refuse to speak."

Crane pressed the issue again, but Ferguson stood firm; he would not answer the question. Finally Crane turned to E. R. Bryan.

"I must insist that the witness tell us who loaned him this money," Crane said to Bryan, "and when it was done."

One of Hanger's assistants, Clarence Martin, protested that this was the governor's private affair, and under the Bill of Rights could not be gone into.

Crane responded that Ferguson had injected the matter into the proceedings by telling about it voluntarily during his direct testimony. Now he was obligated to answer questions about it.

E. R. Bryan asked that he be allowed to postpone a decision until that afternoon. He had not anticipated the question, he said, and was scarcely prepared to make a ruling. So Crane continued with other questions, suggesting that Ferguson had kept the bill increasing the salaries of judges on his desk until the Texas Supreme Court had reached a decision on the "chicken salad" case and that he had called the Beaumont judges who ruled on the Dayton Lumber case "a bunch of ingrates." Ferguson rebuffed both suggestions.

Crane then turned Ferguson over to Chester Terrell, Speaker Fuller's personal counsel, for further questioning.

Terrell covered some of the same ground that Crane had covered, but did bring a few new points: that Ferguson had had a note of $11,000 outstanding at the Temple State Bank when he testified in March that he was no longer in debt to the bank; that he had used his $156,000 loan to repay his debts but still had about $8,000 left; that the governor had appointed an assistant district attorney in San Saba County, even though he had no authority to make such appointments; and that the governor still had possession of about $5,000 in state funds, belonging to the adjutant general's funds and the King's Highway Commission. (The King's Highway is an ancient Spanish road in Texas.)

While Terrell was questioning the governor, one query was put to him from another person on the floor. Had the governor been wearing his glasses when he saw Speaker Fuller vote for Abilene? No, said Ferguson, he had not been wearing his glasses. Terrell would use this against Ferguson later, and it is likely that he arranged for the question to be asked.

Terrell concluded: "Governor, you belong to the Delta Theta Pi Fraternity, don't you?" There was laughter on the floor.

Ferguson: "I don't know what kind of pie it was. It was some kind of pie." More laughter.

That afternoon, E. R. Bryan made his ruling, and in it he agreed totally with M. M. Crane. Governor Ferguson had voluntarily told of the loan; now he must answer all questions that might be asked about it.

One of the governor's supporters stood to appeal the ruling, and so the matter was put to a vote. By a margin of 70 to 56 the Committee of the Whole upheld Bryan's ruling. It was now the expressed will of the Texas House of Representatives that Jim Ferguson must tell who loaned him the $156,000. That night, Jim Ferguson would make no comments for the press.

Wednesday, August 21 — Jim Ferguson returned to the stand and prosecutor Crane came right to the point. He wanted the names of the men who had loaned Jim Ferguson the money.

Ferguson: Without intending any disrespect to the members of the House, he must decline to oblige them.

Crane asked a few more questions, saying that he was doing so only for the record, then acquiesed. He would pursue the matter no further; he would take up other evidence. And so, to the astonishment of everyone, Farmer Jim Ferguson had flatly refused to obey the mandate of the Texas House of Representatives.

Crane read an 1848 statute which required state officials to turn state funds over to the state treasurer. He read a letter from the Board of Regents saying that Dr. Caswell Ellis was authorized to accept offers to assist in the sanitary regulation of school buildings — including San Antonio school buildings — but was not authorized to solicit such offers.

He called a man from Snyder who testified that Secretary Thommason had told him that Speaker Fuller had voted for Snyder.

And he brought Lois McLanahan, a long-distance operator from Cold Springs, to the stand. Miss McLanahan said that she had repeated a conversation between Speaker Fuller and an Abilene reporter, and that Fuller had told the reporter that he had not voted for Abilene.

Then W. A. Hanger had one last go-round with his client. Together, Ferguson and Hanger emphasized certain points: that whatever had been done between the Temple State Bank and other banks had been done without Ferguson's knowledge; that his veto of the judicial salary increase bill had had nothing to do with the decision in the Dayton Lumber Company case; and that he had never told Speaker Fuller that he couldn't vote for Snyder because it had gone against him in the gubernatorial election.

Afterward, Hanger read a letter that Speaker Fuller had written to a man in Fort Worth, saying that if Churchill didn't get the contract to rebuild the San Jacinto County Courthouse, his money would be refunded.

With that, the testimony was ended. Jim Ferguson left the witness stand; no more witnesses would be called.

In contrast to the first three weeks of the House proceedings, with its endless stream of witnesses and their prolonged testimony, events now moved rapidly toward a conclusion.

The Committee of the Whole decided to hold an evening session and to begin final arguments. Each side was allotted equal time, and the arguments were given that night and the following day.

Hanger did not give a final argument; instead Ferguson's case was pleaded by other friends and counsel — Bob Henry, B. Y. Cummings, and Clarence Martin. The principal speech against Ferguson was delivered by Chester Terrell.

Ferguson and Hanger had apparently decided that since they had already spoken so much, other voices might have more influence with the members of the House. Then, too, the final arguments were in a certain sense anticlimatic. For the confrontation between Ferguson and Crane had already had great impact, and many minds were undoubtedly already made up.

Bob Henry, who had served in the U.S. Congress, said that it was not a time for recrimination and abuse. Jim Ferguson had acted in accordance with a policy adopted by the legislature when he disbursed the mansion appropriation. The Canyon City Normal insurance matter had been before the people before — in the March hearings — and had been settled.

The $5,600 charge to the governor's official account had been an error made by a subordinate. In encouraging deposits to his own bank, the governor had followed a long-established custom. On the university question, he had met a difficult situation and dealt with it honestly.

There was no possibility of a mistake in the locating of the new West Texas college, for the testimony of Thommason was indisputable. And the alleged bribe to Speaker Fuller was a bona fide loan, Fuller having given no good reason why Ferguson would want to influence him.

And finally, Jim Ferguson's $2 million appropriation for

the rural schools would be a monument to the future. If there was to be a judgment, let the people render it.

Chester Terrell countered: Ferguson claimed to have seen Fuller write "Abilene" on his ballot, yet he had admitted that he had not been wearing his glasses at the time. The members had seen how careful the governor had been to wear them whenever he had something to read to them while he was on the witness stand.

Terrell referred to Ferguson's claim that if he had been trying to bribe Fuller he would not have given him a check. That was an unfortunate statement, said Terrell, considering the governor's $156,000 loan; no paper had changed hands on that deal.

The governor had said that he knew nothing about the transfer of the Ferguson and Davis notes to the Houston National Exchange Bank, yet they had a letter from T. H. Heard to the Houston bank, saying that Ferguson wanted an extension on the notes.

The governor had testified in March that he had cleared up his indebtedness to the Temple State Bank, when in fact he had guaranteed the notes by which he had cleared up his affairs there, and the notes had been given by men who were financially unable to bear them.

On the matter of the $5,600 charge to the governor's account, that money was even then still in Ferguson's possession. And on the mysterious loan:

"What kind of friends are they who would let the governor, as he says, lose his office and go into bankruptcy rather than disclose their identity? When I have friends like that, I am going to part company with them."

Terrell finished, "Honesty is the basis of democracy. I want you to act, in deciding whether there will be a bill of impeachment considered, in accordance with the law, the constitution, and your conscience."

B. Y. Cummings spoke for the governor: Chester Terrell and Will Hogg were using Speaker Fuller, said Cummings. They were the "priests" and Fuller was the "elder" of the university conspirators.

"You may crucify James E. Ferguson by taking away his office, but there is one thing you cannot do: You cannot take from him the affection of the millions of the common people whose friend he is."

And Clarence Martin took the floor to defend Ferguson, condemning the actions of the prosecution.

"The first act of opposing counsel was to try to call the governor to the stand to testify against himself. When he, the plain outspoken man, told of how his friends had come to his aid in settling his indebtedness, and had told of it voluntarily, they tried to make him divulge the secrets of his inner private life. When the governor refused on his constitutional rights to tell who loaned him the $156,000, they took no step to punish him, so they could keep the record incomplete evidence. . ."

He claimed that keeping state funds in banks was not a crime; it was longtime custom. Perhaps it was a bad custom, but that was no reason to make a scapegoat of James E. Ferguson.

And on the A. and M. matter, who had cast the third ballot for Abilene? The testimony of Thommason was unimpeachable; they couldn't get away from it.

At about 5:00 p.m. on Wednesday, August 22, the final arguments were finished. Now it was time to make a decision. Almost immediately a resolution to report back a bill of impeachment was offered. A Ferguson supporter countered with a proposal to vote on each charge.

At this point, the members of the House who favored impeaching Jim Ferguson faced something of a dilemma, for Speaker Fuller had brought the charges against the governor, and Speaker Fuller had called for the special session to begin with. Yet Fuller had been such an unconvincing, unsettling witness that there was little possibility that his charge that Ferguson had tried to bribe him would be sustained. It would certainly make a contradictory impression on the public if they voted to impeach Jim Ferguson at the same time they rejected Speaker Fuller's very serious personal charge.

The dilemma was easily settled: The motion to vote on

each charge was tabled, and the Committee of the Whole voted on whether to return a bill of impeachment. The vote was in favor of such a bill, 81 to 52.

Chairman Fly was named to head a board of nine managers to draw up the articles of impeachment. The next day, August 23, the managers began their work.

If the Committeee of the Whole had voted on the charges of Speaker Fuller as soon as the final arguments were over, Jim Ferguson's governorship would have ended differently, for as soon as the Texas House presented articles of impeachment to the Senate, the governor would automatically be suspended from office and the lieutenant governor would serve in his place until a judgment was reached by the Senate.

But instead of approving formal articles of impeachment on August 22, the House referred the matter to the board of managers, who did not complete the drafting of the articles until the afternoon of the 24th. So Jim Ferguson continued to hold the power of the governorship for two additional days, and as it happened, he had ample opportunity to exercise that power.

On August 23, Thursday, a race riot broke out in Houston after Houston police had arrested two men of the black 86th Division, which was then stationed in Houston awaiting embarkation to France. After the arrest, black soldiers rioted, and in an insuing melee, twelve people were killed and twenty-one wounded.

At 1:00 a.m. the next morning, Jim Ferguson declared martial law in Houston and dispatched the Texas National Guard to restore order in the city.

Also on Friday the governor issued twenty pardons, including one to a Temple man named Monroe McKelvey, who had been sentenced to ninety-nine years in the penitentiary for the 1912 murder of a Temple barber named Howard.

Finally, late Friday afternoon, the managers returned twenty-one articles of impeachment to the House of Representatives. A vote was taken on each of the articles, and each of them passed, the vote in favor being 70 to 80 on each article, and the vote against numbering 50 to 60.

Nowhere in the articles was there any mention of the governor rigging the voting on the location of West Texas A. and M. or attempting to bribe the speaker of the House. There was, however, an article concerning Jim Ferguson's mysterious loan. The 21 articles:

1. That Ferguson misapplied $5,600 on August 23, 1915, when he used funds from the Canyon City Normal College fire insurance settlement to pay a personal obligation.
2. That he placed the money from the same insurance settlement in the Temple State Bank, where it remained for a year without drawing interest, and to his own profit.
3. That the governor had covered up his indebtedness to the Temple State Bank by transferring two notes of $37,500 each to the Houston National Exchange Bank.
4. That he had attempted to deceive the March investigating committee when testified that he had cleared up his debts to the Temple State Bank, when in fact $75,000 of the money he had paid back was represented by notes on which he himself was guarantor.
5. He had testified in March that he was not indebted to the Temple State Bank when in fact he owed the bank a note payable of $11,200.
6. He had deposited $60,000 in state funds in the Temple State Bank and profited from the deposit.
7. He had assisted in the deposit of $250,000 in state funds to the credit of the Temple State Bank and profited from the transaction.
8. He had sought to have the funds of the Texas Highway Commission deposited in the Temple State Bank.
9. He had deposited state funds in the Temple State Bank and other banks when the state treasury was open to receive them.
10. He had testified in March that he owed the Temple State Bank nothing when in fact he owed it more than the law allowed.
11. He had refused to reveal to the Texas House of Representatives who had loaned him $156,000, which constituted official misconduct.

12. He had diverted funds from the adjutant general's fund and applied to the building of the Canyon City Normal College.

13. He had failed to repay to the state the money he had used to buy groceries and gasoline.

14. He had induced the officers of the Temple State Bank to lend him money in excess of the limit set by law, when he was sworn to uphold the law.

15. He had vetoed the appropriation for the University of Texas, thus setting aside the constitutional provision for the support and maintenance of the university.

16. He had sought to coerce and influence the Board of Regents of the University of Texas to do his autocratic will.

17. He had sought to violate the law by removing members of the Board of Regents without good cause.

18. He had libeled members of the university faculty by calling them liars and grafters without proving his charges.

19. He had sought to influence the chairman of the Board of Regents, Wilbur P. Allen, by remanding a $5,000 bail bond to him.

20. He had improperly sought to influence the courts in matters in which he had a personal interest.

21. He had permitted C. W. Woodman to continue as state labor commissioner after the Texas Senate had refused to confirm his nomination.

After the articles of impeachment had been adopted, it remained only for them to be presented to the Texas Senate. At 9:00 p.m. Fly and the other managers made the presentation, and under the Texas Constitution, Jim Ferguson was automatically suspended from office and replaced by the lieutenant governor.

The next morning, Will Hobby, accompanied by his brother and brother-in-law, called on Jim Ferguson in the governor's office, and a transfer of power was conducted. Hobby invited Ferguson to keep his headquarters in the governor's office until the matter was concluded, and Ferguson accepted the offer. The two men agreed to transfer duties — Hobby would act as governor, Ferguson as lieutenant governor, but of course Ferguson would have few if any official duties left.

Hobby was a 45-year-old newspaperman from Houston who had first run for office in the 1914 campaign for the lieutenant governorship. An hour after his meeting with Ferguson, he performed his first official duty as acting governor by signing a request of the governor of Michigan to return to Texas a man wanted in DeWitt County on charges of forgery.

That evening, the secretary of the Texas Senate, John D. McCall, delivered to Jim Ferguson a summons to appear before the bar of the Texas Senate at 10:00 a.m. the following Wednesday, August 29, to answer the articles of impeachment that had been preferred against him by the House of Representatives.

Under the Texas Constitution, the Texas Senate would try the case as a High Court of Impeachment.

4

The High Court of Impeachment

The Texas Constitution requires that the Texas Senate be under oath when sitting as a High Court of Impeachment, and the senators decided to invite the chief justice of the Texas Supreme Court, John Nelson Phillips, to come to Austin to swear them in. Phillips was reached in North Texas by long distance telephone — a fact that was considered newsworthy by the reporters covering the impeachment — and agreed to come to Austin, but he arrived one day late, so the trial could not begin until August 30.

In the interval between the proceedings of the House and trial before the Senate, Jim Ferguson refunded some money to the state. He gave back $2,403 that he had spent for groceries and he gave $3,116 in Texas National Guard funds to Acting Governor Hobby, who turned it into the state treasurer.

On August 28 the Senate voted not to confirm Ferguson's last two appointments to the University of Texas Board of Regents and instead confirmed a nominee submitted by Acting Governor Hobby — George W. Brackenridge, a longtime university supporter and benefactor. The acting governor took another official step as well: since the special session of the legislature would expire at the end of the month, he had to call for another special session to convene September 1, in order to insure Jim Ferguson's trial.

A committee of the Senate had already been preparing the rules of evidence and procedure that would be used in the trial. The senators had decided that they would not take a record of the proceedings of the House; instead, each charge would be heard in

M. M. CRANE, a former lieutenant governor of Texas, prosecuted Ferguson before the House of Representatives and the Senate, which tried Ferguson as a High Court of Impeachment. Crane had also served as attorney general in the 1890s, and had won fame by prosecuting anti-trust cases against big oil companies. He met Ferguson in head-on confrontations before both the House and Senate, and both times came out the victor. At the time, he was in private practice in Dallas.

— *Photo from Texas State Library*

its own right as though it were new. The Senate planned to be guided by the format used in the 1913 impeachment trial of New York Governor William Sulzer.

On August 29, the House of Representatives voted to hire M. M. Crane to prosecute Ferguson before the Texas Senate and to pay him $1,250 for his services, the same sum he had received for investigating Ferguson before the House.

One member offered a resolution calling for Crane to be held in contempt of the House and required to forfeit his fee for failing to obey the House and force Jim Ferguson to reveal who had loaned him the $156,000, but the resolution was rejected.

On August 30, John Nelson Phillips swore in the Texas Senate, beginning with the president pro tem, W. L. Dean, and the trial began.

Jim Ferguson and his counsel were escorted to a table facing the chairman, and W. A. Hanger was allowed to respond to the charges preferred by the House.

There had been speculation as to whether Hanger's response would take the form of a demurrer or a motion to quash. A demurrer is a plea for dismissal on grounds that the accusation, though it may be true, does not constitute an offense. A motion to quash is a request for dismissal on various legal grounds — for instance because a jury was unfairly selected or because the statute of limitations has expired or because there is an improper joinder of defendants.

The speculation ended now as Hanger read a 6,000-word demurrer.

None of the articles of impeachment, said Hanger, constituted high crimes and misdemeanors, or a violation of Ferguson's oath, or official misconduct. They were not grounds for impeachment.

Further, some of the charges referred to events that had occured during the governor's first term in office, before the previous election. The governor could not now be impeached for something he had done in a previous term.

And further still, the House of Representatives had no right to take up the question of impeaching the governor at a special session that had been called for a specific, different purpose. In other words, the articles of impeachment were unconstitutional.

Surprisingly, Hanger made no effort to persuade the Senate to rule on his demurrer, and later in the day Crane told reporters that the Senate would not pass on the issues raised by the demurrer until it voted on the articles of impeachment, or at least until after testimony had been taken.

After Hanger had read the demurrer, the Senate adjourned until the following Monday in order for process to be served. Some senators at first objected to the postponement, but Crane assured them that it was in the best interests of justice, and so they agreed to it.

On Sunday, September 2, most of the newspapers in Texas carried an open letter from Jim Ferguson to the people of Texas, asking that he be given a fair and impartial hearing. Ferguson wrote that whatever profit he had gained from the funds in the Temple State Bank had been small, and he had been ''foremost in looking after education and promoting constructive legislation.''

Monday, September 3 — The morning session was taken up with the reading of the articles of impeachment and the demurrer that had been offered by Hanger; that afternoon, testimony finally began.

M. M. Crane called his first witness, and once again, as it had been before the House of Representatives, the first witness was the assistant cashier of the Temple State Bank, Henry Blum.

Under Crane's questioning, Blum outlined Jim Ferguson's indebtedness to the bank throughout the years 1915 and 1916. He read lists of Ferguson's withdrawals and charges, including the $5,600 charge of August 23, 1915. He conceded that there was no memorandum to show to whom the money had been paid, and admitted that the memorandum had probably been returned to the governor along with his bank statement.

Blum volunteered the information that the statements were mailed to the governor's secretary, J. H. Davis. This angered the prosecutor.

''Why did you say that?'' demanded Crane. ''No one asked you for that information.''

Blum returned to the stand on Tuesday and was asked to read lists of the state's deposits in his bank, lists of notes Governor Ferguson owed the bank, lists of all the loans the bank had made.

His response revealed that the secretary of state's account remained in the bank for eight months instead of three, as Ferguson had claimed; that balances of state funds had reached $760,411; that the bank had outstanding loans and deposits in other banks totaling $522,000 when it had only $45,000 in cash on hand.

Crane: Then didn't it appear that the bank had used state funds to make its loans?

Blum: No, they couldn't loan out state money. Deposits in other banks were not considered loans.

Crane went back over the figures and demonstrated that even if the bank had used all of its resources, it still could not have made all the loans that it had outstanding. Blum then admitted that perhaps some of the state's funds had been used for loans.

He made other admissions as well: that it had been necessary at times to use state funds to make good on the bank's daily balances, that even since settling his affairs, Jim Ferguson had held more than the legal limit of the bank's funds, that Jim Ferguson had personally guaranteed three notes of $37,500 each that he had used in 1917 to settle his indebtedness.

W. A. Hanger cross-examined Blum and asked him about Ferguson's relationship with the bank. Since taking office, said Blum, the governor had severed all official connection with the bank. He had nothing to do with its management.

Hanger produced a check, which Blum said had been charged to the governor's special account when it should have been charged to his official account— the check was for $6,156. Here was an error that had worked to the governor's disadvantage rather than to his favor.

And Blum testified that if the $5,600 charge of August 15

had been charged to the governor's personal account (the one with $50 in it), it would have been paid; it would simply have meant an overdraft on which the governor would have been charged interest.

Hanger: Had the Temple State Bank ever failed to honor a check on state funds?

Blum: No, never. State checks had always been honored, even when they had been for as much as $230,000.

Finally, Hanger read a letter that Governor Ferguson had written to the directors of the bank in January, 1917, expressing his desire to settle his affairs with the bank.

On re-examination, Crane challenged the $6,156 check that had supposedly worked to the governor's disadvantage. The check had been charged to his personal account on December 8, 1915, but had been replaced on December 31. As for the famous $5,600, it had never been replaced.

Then Crane read a series of letters that Ferguson had written to the officers of the bank in which the governor made suggestions and directed business deals. All of the letters had been written while Ferguson was governor.

Crane's final witness was Henry Fox of the Houston National Exchange Bank, who testified that his bank had taken over the $37,500 notes at the request of the governor. T. H. Heard of the Temple State Bank had arranged the details.

Wednesday, September 5 — Crane called an official from the Union National Bank of Houston, who testified that the Texas Penitentiary Commission had kept large balances in his bank and that Jim Ferguson had tried to borrow $30,000, but his loan application had been rejected. The governor had kept an official account in the bank but had withdrawn it in April, 1916, after the loan had been rejected.

But defense counsel Hanger brought out that Ferguson had been a longtime customer of the bank and had influenced the Union National to loan the Penitentiary Commission $120,000 without security so that the crops on the prison farms could be harvested. The governor had not been angry when his loan was rejected, and his relations with the bank were still cordial. The

Penitentiary Commission's largest deposits had come after Ferguson's loan request had been turned down.

Crane called Carl Widen of the American National Bank of Austin, who described Governor Ferguson's official account at his bank, saying that deposits in it had reached $103,000. Widen did not know which state funds were represented by the deposits.

Crane then asked questions about Ferguson's deposits in the current year, and observers assumed that he was trying to find some trace of the governor's mysterious loan.

Widen explained that Ferguson had deposited $11,000 in February and $40,000 in April; another $25,000 had been deposited to the credit of the Houston National Exchange Bank.

Had Widen noticed the wrappers around the currency? Yes, much of it had been bound in the wrappers of the Alamo National Bank of San Antonio.

On cross-examination, Hanger elicited that Widen had never seen Jim Ferguson actually make a deposit. Then he asked if other state officials had accounts in the American National.

Crane objected to the question, and President Pro Tem Dean sustained the objection. Evidence that other officials had violated the law would in no way excuse the governor, said Dean. He would not allow the question.

But Hanger protested that he wasn't trying to show that other officials had violated the law. He was trying to show that other officials, and Jim Ferguson asa well, had followed a legal policy by keeping accounts in the American National. Dean reversed himself; the question would be permitted.

Widen then answered that the general land office, the attorney general, the state comptroller and the secretary of state all had collection accounts in his bank.

And didn't the University of Texas have an account there? Yes, Was it checked out monthly? No.

At the outset of the afternoon session, Crane sought to introduce as evidence a letter that Ferguson had written to the state banking commissioner, a letter that Crane had submitted during the proceedings of the House. But Hanger objected to the letter being introduced, and a legal skirmish ensued on a principle that has an important bearing on the general law of impeachment. The way the Texas Senate handled this question is one of the reasons the Ferguson impeachment is an important precedent in the law of impeachment.

Hanger objected to the letter, citing Texas *criminal* law, on grounds that a respondent could not have his testimony from one trial introduced against him in another trial that would in any way tend to injure him.

Crane countered, citing Texas *civil* law, that the evidence of any voluntary or involuntary witness could indeed be used against him.

The question was, was this a criminal or a civil proceeding? The answer would determine if Crane could introduce the letter, as well as other of Ferguson's testimony before the House; and also whether, perhaps, Crane could call Ferguson to the witness stand before the High Court of Impeachment.

Hanger's assistant, Bob Henry, interjected that when he had been in the U.S. Congress during the impeachment of Judge Swayne, the Congress had held that such letters were inadmissable. Crane retorted that acts of the U.S. Congress did not determine the procedure to be used in state courts.

Hanger insisted that the present trial was a criminal proceeding and cited the Texas Constitution, which refers to ''all criminal proceedings excepting treason and impeachment.'' But Crane argued that the punishment to be inflicted determined the nature of a case. In this instance, removal from office, and possible disbarment from further office, dictated that the trial was a civil matter.

The president pro tem made a ruling: he would permit Crane to read the letter as evidence, but the question of the admissability of Ferguson's testimony before the House would remain open, to be decided as individual instances arose. For now, he would not rule as to whether this was a civil or a criminal trial, but later he would have to.

Later Crane called a succession of witnesses from the American National Bank — two vice presidents and the first receiving teller — all of whom he asked about the wrappers in which Jim Ferguson's recently deposited currency had been bound. Most of it had been in the wrappers of the Alamo National Bank of San Antonio, but some had been in the wrappers of a Dallas Federal Reserve Bank; one bundle had come from a Houston bank. Not much could be made of this, said the first receiving teller. After all, the currency could have passed through intervening banks.

Lastly, Crane called the Texas Highway Commissioner, Curtiss Hancock, who testified that after he assumed his office, Governor Ferguson had suggested that he clear the commission's voluminous checks through the Temple State Bank. Hancock had taken the suggestion as a friendly offer to help him dispose of large amounts of paper, but the commission had never made any deposits in the Temple State Bank.

On Thursday, Crane began by calling P. L. Downs of the First National Bank in Temple, who again described Jim Ferguson's $5,000 note payment of August 20, 1915. With interest, the payment had been for $5,600, and although the credit slip showed August 20, the charge-off had not been made until the twenty-first. Settlement had been made by the Temple State Bank.

Then for the rest of the day, and continuing into Friday, Crane called a series of witnesses to discuss Governor Ferguson's dealings with the Board of Regents of the University of Texas.

First, Regent W. R. Brents testified about Ferguson's relationship with the board and with the university's president, Robert L. Vinson. On the day Brents was appointed, Ferguson asked him if he thought Vinson had enough backbone to run the university.

Brents: "I told him that I thought Dr. Vinson had plenty of backbone."

Brents told of the May 28 meeting of the Board of Regents that had been broken up by the demonstration of the University of Texas students. The governor had been very indignant and had said that he ought not to turn the appropriation over "to that mob out there."

Later Vinson had been called before the regents and had told them that although he had suspended classes for the day, he had known nothing about the student demonstration. Afterward, Governor Ferguson had again insisted that Vinson, as well as Mr. Lomax and Professors Coffer, Ellis, Mayes, Battle, Potts and Mathes had to be fired. He would veto the appropriation if the men were not let go. Brents suggested that Ferguson let the Board of Regents handle the matter, but Ferguson bluntly responded that he didn't need any advice.

After Brents' direct testimony, the prosecution read a letter that Ferguson had written to him, chastising Brents for voting not to seat one of Ferguson's later appointees to the Board of Regents. Brents had no right to do that, Ferguson had said in the letter, reminding Brents of his promise to cooperate. Brents had replied that he knew of no better way to cooperate than to conscientiously perform his duty.

On cross-examination, W. A. Hanger asked Brents if Governor Ferguson had known that Brents favored Dr. Vinson when he appointed him to the board. No, said Brents, the governor's only concern then had been the remedying of certain abuses at the university, including abuses by fraternities and the charging of mileage books at full price by professors.

Brents explained for Hanger that the meeting of the regents had been broken up by the noise of the student demonstration, and that the regents, when they investigated the incident, had questioned only faculty members and not students.

Crane's next move was to read a letter that Ferguson had written to another regent, Rabbi Faber, asking that Faber resign from the Board of Regents if he could not cooperate with Ferguson. Faber's reply had been that he had not known that Ferguson wanted a marionette, and that he would not resign.

Crane then had Ferguson's proclamation removing Regent S. J. Jones from the board, as well as a series of telegrams that had passed between the governor and Regent C. E. Kelly of El Paso; in one telegram, Ferguson insisted that Kelly come to the board meeting in Galveston, as he was badly needed.

Then Crane called Representative Dudley of El Paso, who testified about a meeting that he and El Paso's senator had had with Governor Ferguson, in which they had tried to recommend various El Paso men for appointment to the Board of Regents. Ferguson had rebuffed them, telling them that he had a man in El Paso who "would stand hitched and do what I tell him to do." Ferguson had been referring to C. E. Kelly, whom he had subsequently appointed to the board.

Crane next read the proclamation by which Ferguson had remitted the $5,000 bail bond to Wilbur P. Allen. Then he called a man named Franz Fiset to testify as to how Allen's attitude toward President Vinson had changed after Ferguson had remitted the bond.

Hanger objected to the testimony, saying that it was only hearsay evidence, but he was overruled.

Fiset explained that Allen had once told him that President Vinson was an excellent man who had made an outstanding start at the university; but after Governor Ferguson remitted Allen's bail bond, Allen told Fiset that President Vinson was incompetent and unfit.

Crane then called the chief clerk of the secretary of state's office and had him read Jim Ferguson's veto of the University of Texas appropriation bill. Then he called a former regent, J. W. Butler, to the stand.

Butler testified that he had sought appointment to the Board of Regents because he wanted to help Dr. Vinson. He was a longtime friend of both Vinson and Governor Ferguson, and he wanted to see the two men cooperate and get along with each other.

On the day of the student demonstration, however, it was apparent that the two men had grown far apart and that a reconciliation was unlikely. The day after the demonstration, Governor Ferguson told Butler that it would be embarrassing for him to continue, so Butler offered to resign, and the governor accepted his offer.

Crane asked if Ferguson had deposited any money in Butler's bank—Butler owned a bank in Clifton, a small town in Bosque County, where Ferguson had his ranch — and Butler replied that Ferguson had deposited $7,500 in May.

On cross-examination, Butler admitted that the governor

had always expressed a desire to do what was best for the university. Also, faculty members had told the regents that they had been powerless to stop the parade; and after the episode, Butler had asked President Vinson to apologize to the governor and try to improve their relations, but Vinson had declined.

Crane then called the president of the University of Texas himself, Robert E. Vinson, and Vinson testified for the remainder of the Friday session and into Saturday.

Vinson had been president of the Southwest Presbyterian Seminary in Austin before his surprise election to the presidency of the University of Texas, and Crane's first question was to ask Vinson how many sermons he had preached since assuming his new role.

Eight or nine, answered Vinson.

What was the nature of the sermons?

Hanger objected that question: it was irrelevant to the articles of impeachment, he said. The objection was sustained.

Saturday, September 8 — Over repeated objections, some of which resulted in votes by the Senate on whether or not to allow certain questions, Crane directed Vinson to discuss the professors of the University of Texas — their salaries, their work loads, and so on. They worked longer hours than professors at similar schools, said Vinson. They had to write books, prepare for classes, grade papers: their schedules were rigorous.

Vinson described for Crane the October 1916 meeting of the Board of Regents at which Jim Ferguson presented his charges against the faculty members, insisting that they be dismissed promptly, without a hearing. The regents had refused to obey the governor's wishes, instead insisting that the men must be given a full hearing, and the regents later appealed to the Texas legislature to fully investigate the situation at the university.

Later, in a conference with the Senate committee that conducted the investigation, one senator had proposed to Vinson that he strike a compromise with the governor: Vinson would obtain the resignations of the professors, and Ferguson would sign the appropriation bill. Vinson told the senator that that would be impossible: the regents had already taken the matter out of his hands.

Crane asked if Wilbur P. Allen had ever expressed any preference for Vinson as president of the university, and Vinson replied that Allen had been to his home during the March investigation of Governor Ferguson and had made complimentary statements to him. Crane then asked about the meeting the two men had on June 6, when Allen supposedly tried to persuade Vinson to resign. Allen had told him that he had no deal with the governor, said Vinson, but that if he would resign, Allen was certain that he could persuade Ferguson to approve at least $1 million of the appropriation. Vinson had declined.

In answer to other questions, Vinson explained that he had excused the university students from their classes on May 28, the day of the Board of Regents meeting in the governor's office, so that they could hold a rally and draw up resolutions. He had known nothing about the parade and had not intended to offend the governor.

He did not know why Jim Ferguson wanted the professors fired. He did know that one of Ferguson's objections to Dean Mayes of the Journalism department was that Mayes had — in Ferguson's words— "skinned him from hell to breakfast" in his newspaper.

"I never use such language," smiled the university president, "but I can quote it." Even Jim Ferguson got a laugh out of that one.

Vinson stated that more than 300 university students had been accepted at the officer training camp at Leon Springs. (This included some members of the university's football team, most of whom had left the campus along with Coach Gene Van Gent to enlist in the American Expeditionary Force.)

The effect of Ferguson's veto of the appropriation? It would have caused the college to close, answered Vinson, and the faculty to disband; it would have required a new organization and a fresh start.

Cross-examining, W. A. Hanger asked Vinson to identify the university budget, then challenged him about some of the items that were in it, including the outside work that had been done by Dr. Ellis. Had Vinson approved the outside work? As far as Vinson knew, Dr. Ellis had not done any outside work since Vinson had become president; but Vinson didn't disapprove of any work Ellis had done with the permission of the Board of Regents.

Had Vinson tried to stop the student parade on May 28? Vinson had not seen the parade, and no, he had not tried to stop it.

Crane called R. S. Sterling, the president of the Dayton Lumber Company. Sterling explained that he had bought 3,260 acres of timberland from Ferguson and another man, but litigation had arisen over the title to the land, and while the litigation was in process, the proceeds of the timber cut on the land had been placed in an escrow account in the Temple State Bank. Sterling had never given Ferguson permission to use the money in the account.

The next witness also had an interest in the timberland. This was H. P. Mansfield, who testified that two weeks ago he had sued Governor Ferguson for his share of the escrow account, since the court had finally held that it belonged to the lumber company, and not to Ferguson.

Monday, September 10 — Crane began by introducing letters that Governor Ferguson had written to the courts — one to the Texas Supreme Court prior to its decision on the chicken salad case, and one to the Beaumont Court of Civil Appeals, urging the court to decide in Ferguson's favor in the Dayton Lumber Company case. Then he introduced the proclamation by which Ferguson had vetoed the judicial salary increase bill.

Crane returned to Friday's line of inquiry and called H. P. Mansfield's attorney, a lawyer from Houston named Kittrell. Kittrell testified that Ferguson had been very indignant a few weeks back when Kittrell had asked him for an accounting of the Dayton Lumber funds; the governor had told Kittrell that he couldn't have an accounting until after the impeachment proceedings were finished.

Crane brought a series of newspaper reporters to the stand

to identify and describe articles they had written about Ferguson's speeches condemning the University of Texas professors. Clarence Dubose of the *Dallas News* related Ferguson's Walnut Springs speech, in which he called the university professors "corruptionists and butterfly chasers." Another reporter described a speech Ferguson had given in West Texas, in which he had said that members of the faculty were guilty of more disloyalty than the FLPAs. (Certain members of the Farmers and Laborers Protective Association had been charged with conspiracy to evade the draft.)

Then came F. A. Gross, the Houston building contractor who had rebuilt the Canyon City Normal College. Gross testified that he had had great difficulty collecting the estimates that he submitted monthly to the state. He often had to come to Austin and see Governor Ferguson personally in order to collect the payment. The final payment had been in the form of a deficiency warrant; Gross had given up on ever collecting the money and had finally sold the warrant to a bank for less than its face value.

Crane asked him to explain how that could have happened. Gross replied that he had come to Austin to see Governor Ferguson and collect the money that was due him, and Ferguson sent him to the state comptroller, who issued him a warrant. Gross took the warrant to the state treasurer's office, only to discover that there were no funds in the state treasury with which to pay the warrant, so Gross went back to see Ferguson once again. The governor told him that he would send a check over to the state treasury, so Gross returned to the treasurer's office. This time he was told that the governor's check had been placed in the general revenue account and that there still were no funds available to pay his warrant. At that point Gross gave up and discounted the warrant to a bank.

On cross-examination, Hanger asked if Gross did not know that the funds he needed had been readily available at the American National Bank. Gross answered that he only knew that he always had to come to Austin to collect his money.

Didn't he know that Governor Ferguson had the money to pay him, even if the state treasury did not? Yes, Gross knew that.

Wasn't it true that the funds Ferguson had were allocated for the main building only, and hadn't Gross been trying to collect on expenses he had incurred in building a wing? No, said Gross, the main building alone cost $100,000 — the amount the governor had — the wing cost an additional $60,000.

Gross's story was substantiated by a clerk from the state treasurer's office and an officer of the Texas Trust Company of Austin. The clerk testified that often in 1915 and 1916 there had been no funds in the treasury with which to pay warrants. As funds became available, warrants were called in.

Crane: "If the funds in the Temple State Bank had been in the state treasury, would there have been enough on hand to pay the warrants?"

Answer: "Yes, if the funds in the Temple State had been in the treasury, the Gross warrants as well as others would have been paid."

W. A. Hanger challenged the clerk over the check that Governor Ferguson had sent over to pay Gross's warrant. The clerk explained that checks of that kind were placed in the general revenue, then Gross and others were paid in the normal course of paying warrants.

But this wasn't tax money, was it? What authority was there, under law, for placing a special fund in the general revenue? The clerk was befuddled: as far as he knew there was none.

A. A. Turner of the Texas Trust Company testified that his bank had bought two groups of warrants from Gross, each group totaling about $14,000, and had charged Gross $190. The company had later collected on the warrants. Part of the payment had been for the main building and part for the wing.

Tuesday, September 11 — Speaker Pro Tem Dean allowed M. M. Crane to introduce the testimony that State Comptroller Terrell had given before the House investigating committee in March. The testimony concerned a contract that Governor Ferguson had with an Austin man named Achilles, under which Achilles agreed to supply Ferguson with groceries, automobile accessories and other items and to present the governor with a monthly bill, which Ferguson would pay out of the mansion light and fuel fund. After reading Terrell's testimony, Crane read a long list of deficiency warrants that Ferguson had issued to Achilles during 1916.

Crane then proposed to read a list of "admissions" that Governor Ferguson had made, both during the March investigation and the impeachment proceedings of the House. Hanger strongly objected, once again on the grounds that Texas law prohibited a defendant's testimony in one proceeding being used against him in another. The old argument of whether this was a criminal trial or not came up again.

Crane insisted that it was not: "I find that most impeachment proceedings in other states are considered criminal cases, but I do not believe that this applies in Texas." He argued that the punishment decided the nature of a case, and in this instance — removal from office and possible prevention from holding further office — did not even constitute punishment at all: It was simply a measure to protect the public.

W. A. Hanger rebutted: "I undertake to say that opposing counsel cannot find a single action of this sort which has not been found to be a criminal procedure."

Hanger read from the Texas Constitution, which calls for the lieutenant governor to act as governor during impeachment proceedings until the governor is acquitted or if impeached, until a successor is elected.

"I undertake to say that if the framers of our law had not regarded an impeachment trial as a criminal procedure, they would never have used that word 'acquitted.' "

He read another portion of the constitution stating that no person "shall be convicted for a criminal offense unless on the indictment of a grand jury, except in cases of impeachment."

After more arguing, President Pro Tem Dean settled the matter by making a final ruling: The testimony was admissable; first because the present case was not a criminal case but rather a "quasi-criminal" case, and second, even if it were a criminal case, the governor could not, having voluntarily testified before the House, now claim immunity before the Senate.

Wednesday, September 12 — Crane read into the record a list of confessions and statements that Ferguson had previously made:

— His statement in March that he would repay the amount of the mansion funds that he had misused if the Texas Supreme Court ruled against him in the chicken salad case.

— His statement before the House that he would loan a man $100,000 if he considered the man safe, even though the law forbade a bank to loan more than 30 percent of its capital and surplus to one person.

— His reply to Crane that he knew that every court in the state was against him on the expenditure matter.

— His admission that he had taken the Canyon City Normal College insurance settlement money from banks where it was drawing interest and placed it in banks where it did not, including his own bank.

— His admission that his special account in the Temple State Bank could not have been used to pay his $5,600 loan payment on August 23, 1915, because the money was being held in escrow until certain litigation was concluded.

— His declaration that he would not tell who had loaned him the $156,000 with which he had settled his financial affairs.

Crane was interrupted by a senator who wanted to know why the House had not taken steps to punish Ferguson for refusing to tell who had loaned him the money, and Crane replied that he would be happy to answer the question, but an objection from the floor kept him from doing so. The senator appealed, but the ensuing vote went against him. Crane went on to other admissions:

— Ferguson's statement that he had suggested that the secretary of state deposit funds in the Temple State Bank and that Ferguson wanted the deposits to be as large as possible.

— His admission that he still owed $5,000 to his official account in the Temple State Bank.

When Crane had finished, W. A. Hanger asked for a recess, and that night he and Ferguson met for a strategy session. They no doubt recognized that Crane was about to rest his case and were trying to decide how they would present Ferguson's defense.

Thursday, September 12 — Crane opened by reading a few letters from Ferguson to the Temple State Bank, but they revealed little that was new, and he called Henry Blum again to let him identify still other letters, then he was finished. M. M. Crane rested the prosecution and yielded to W. A. Hanger.

Hanger called the first defense witness, Frank Hargon, a cashier in the state department, who explained that $5,000 of the state department funds deposited in the Temple State Bank were an accumulation of excess remittances to the state department, which did not belong in the state treasury.

Hanger produced a record that Hargon had earlier prepared, showing that $250,000 of the state department's funds had remained in the Temple State Bank only forty-five days.

Hanger called Henry S. Fox of the Houston National Exchange Bank, who explained that Mr. Mansfield, the man who had testified about suing Jim Ferguson for an accounting of the Dayton Lumber Company escrow account, owed the Houston National $6,000 and had used his contract with the governor as security.

Then J. H. Davis, the governor's personal secretary, took the stand. Davis testified that Governor Ferguson had known nothing about the $5,600 charge to his official account. The bank statement had come to Davis, and he had simply noted the charge and locked the statement in a safe. It had never occurred to him that an error might have been made, and he never called the matter to the governor's attention. Ferguson only learned of the matter when he was called before the grand jury.

Friday, September 14 — Hanger recalled Davis to the stand, but not until he had first read a couple of items into the record. First was Ferguson's message to the Texas Senate in January of 1917, calling attention to the King's Highway funds that he had in his possession; the second was a letter to the state treasurer that Ferguson had written in the interum between the proceedings of the House and the Senate trial, by which he had refunded certain monies to the state, and pointing out that he promised to refund the money if the legislature asked him to do so.

Then Hanger questioned Davis about a letter Davis had

written to the Temple State Bank, sending it along with a $5,081 check from a Kansas City bank, the check serving as the initial deposit of the Canyon City Normal insurance funds. In the letter, Davis cautioned the bank not to increase the loans on the strength of the deposit; and Davis now told Hanger that he had been referring to the entire Canyon Normal account and not just the initial deposit.

On cross-examination, M. M. Crane turned Davis into a more effective witness for the prosecution than he had been for the defense. First Davis admitted that some forty letters between Ferguson and the Temple State Bank had been introduced as evidence during the impeachment proceedings.

Crane wanted to know why Ferguson asked for statements of his various accounts if he did not look after his own affairs, and Davis conceded that Ferguson did in fact look after some of his own affairs.

Now Crane reviewed the record of the Canyon Normal deposits and withdrawals and reconstructed the history of the account. Using accounting methods, he proved that a $5,600 shortage in the Canyon City Normal account was eventually reflected as the King's Highway funds in the governor's account, along with an overdraft of $1,850 in the governor's account in the American National Bank of Austin. The accounting was complicated; Davis admitted that Crane was correct. Crane then took up the matter of Jim Ferguson's mysterious loan.

Davis insisted that he knew nothing about the $156,000, except for the fact that the governor had given him $40,000 to deposit in the American National Bank.

Crane produced a deposit slip by which Ferguson had deposited $35,000 in cash in the Temple State Bank in April. Davis claimed that he knew nothing about such batches of currency, save for the $40,000 he had already mentioned.

Crane: "Who gave the money to the governor?"

Davis: "I don't know."

Crane: "Did you see anyone with the governor before he gave you the $40,000?"

Davis: "I did not."

To further questions, Davis answered that he had not noticed the wrappers around the currency the governor gave him; yes, his note for $37,500 was really Ferguson's; he had learned about the $5,600 error when he testified before the grand jury.

What had he told the grand jury?

Hanger objected to the question, and Dean told Crane to withhold the question until Dean could consult legal authorities as to whether or not the question was allowable. After Crane released Davis, the High Court adjourned until Monday.

Monday, September 17 — Anyone who listens to Jim Ferguson must recognize that the governor believes that he is completely innocent; he does not think he has done anything wrong. And whether from vanity or obstinancy, Ferguson for some reason believes that he is the best person to convince his colleagues of that.

Shortly after 10:00 a.m., after some brief testimony from J. H. Davis, W. A. Hanger called Jim Ferguson to the stand. Despite the fact that this tactic had backfired in the proceedings of the House (the question of the $156,000 loan had come up only because Ferguson testified himself), Hanger was prepared to again make Jim Ferguson his chief defense witness.

Ferguson began by telling the Senate the story of his life — his childhood as the son of a Methodist minister, quitting school at sixteen, his years as a laborer and railroad man, finally returning home to Bell County and his widowed mother. He studied law, gained admission to the bar in 1897, and practiced law in Belton. Eventually, he said, he had drifted into banking, moved to Temple and organized the Temple State Bank.

Finally he had been stung by the political bee and been elected governor of Texas; since he had become governor, it had been one problem after another. Because of all the problems he had been so busy that he put in more hours performing his duties than any other man in Austin, and that included the black porters. He didn't have time to look after his own affairs because he was so busy; he left his banking matters to C. A. Hughes and his personal affairs to J. H. Davis.

After Ferguson finished his self-pitying talk, he and Hanger began a rebuttal of the charges, just as they had done before the House. Hanger prompted his client by reading the articles of impeachment, and Ferguson responded. They talked the rest of today and into tomorrow, beginning with the matter of the Canyon City Normal College insurance funds.

When he became governor, said Ferguson, the contract to rebuild the school had already been let, so he couldn't loan the money out to draw interest; it had to be subject to check at any time. There was no reason for Gross to discount the warrants; Ferguson had written checks to cover them promptly. The checks represented a special fund, and he couldn't understand why the state treasurer had put them into the general revenue.

He never knew about the $5,600 charge against his official account until he testified before the Travis County Grand Jury. There was no reason for the error. Even his personal account had been insufficient, if the matter had been brought to his attention, he would have taken care of it. His credit was good, shown by the fact that he later borrowed over $100,000. He didn't know that the $5,600 had gone to settle his personal obligation. He had never intended to profit from the Canyon City Normal funds; he had just wanted to keep them handy. Ferguson astonished the senators and spectators as he fervently denied the allegation.

I call upon the God of Heaven to strike me dead before this assembly if I do not speak the truth when I say that I never intended to make a nickel, even a cent, off the money in the Temple State Bank.

How anyone could think that he would sell his honor and his official position for the small profit that would come to him was something he couldn't understand.

It was true that he had settled his overline at the Temple State Bank with four notes of $37,500 each. By the time of the March investigation, his own note had been paid, but Ferguson knew that if left the others in the Temple State, there would be gossip and the bank would be injured. So he had arranged with Henry Fox for the Houston National Exchange Bank to take over the notes of his brother A. F. Ferguson and J. H. Davis. But he

ROBERT E. VINSON, president of the University of Texas, refused to resign just to mollify Governor Ferguson. Vinson had been a surprise selection to head the university, after serving as president of a Presbyterian seminary in Austin. Ferguson never approved of the appointment. Vinson served as president of the university for seven years, enhancing the quality of the school and acquiring important book collections for its library.

— Photo from Baker Texas History Center,
University of Texas, Austin

didn't know that T. H. Heard had arranged for the Houston bank to keep the notes for only fifteen or twenty days. He had originally borrowed the money to cover political expenses and to buy cattle.

He didn't realize that some of his small notes were still outstanding when he testified in March that he didn't owe any money to the Temple State Bank.

The secretary of state's account had not remained in the Temple bank long enough to make loans on the money. As for any interest that the American National Bank might have paid to the Temple State, that thought had never occurred to him.

He had not asked Curtiss Hancock to make deposits in the Temple State Bank so he could profit from them. He was just trying to be helpful; Hancock's checks had been piling up. The law requiring state funds to be placed in the state treasury did not prevent them from being deposited in banks: Every state official had a bank account.

He had called the special session only obstensibly to consider the university appropriation. In fact he had called it to show that he was not going to run away from the impeachment proceedings.

He had not sought to set aside the constitution in his dealings with the University of Texas. He had only suggested that the faculty members be let out because he didn't think they were proper persons to be in charge of young people.

Hanger didn't bring up the matter of the $156,000 loan, and Ferguson didn't volunteer to talk about it. After the High Court adjourned Monday, newspaper reporters were speculating that one outcome of the affair might be for the court to recess until Jim Ferguson agreed to tell who had loaned him the money. Contempt proceedings might be undertaken. A recess for such a reason would have the effect of making Will Hobby governor of Texas until the next election.

Tuesday, September 18—The governor and his lawyer continued their response to the articles of impeachment, once again avoiding the matter of Jim Ferguson's famous loan. Ferguson defended his veto of the university appropriation.

In the first place, he thought the appropriation was extravagant, but he had also been influenced by the student "mob" that gathered to "browbeat" him. That was done with the knowledge of the faculty, he was certain of it.

Further, an unreasonable injunction had been brought, one that interferred with the regents' right to run the affairs of the university. (Ferguson was referring to the injunction obtained by the university's secretary, John Lomax, preventing the regents from firing anyone during their meeting at Galveston.)

He had never removed regents without good cause. He wasn't against higher education, provided that the cost wasn't too high. He had never tried to close the university: with economy measures and issuance of deficiency warrants, it could have remained in operation. He had only wanted to serve notice to the faculty that the regents were going to run things at the school.

On the matter of charging the faculty with disloyalty, Ferguson read an article from the student newspaper, *The Daily Texan.* The article reported that certain voters in Austin had scratched Ferguson's name off the last primary ballot and replaced it with the name of P. Lender, a Negro. Ferguson:

"Any person who would countenance in any way an act by which a Negro would be shown preference over the white nominee of the Democratic Party in Texas is guilty of disloyalty."

This was a strange statement coming from a man who would someday become the bitter opponent and chief nemesis of the Ku Klux Klan. And it is certain that this sort of outlandish statement did not convince anyone that the faculty of the University of Texas was guilty of "disloyalty."

Ferguson responded to other charges. It was totally untrue that he had tried to influence Wilbur P. Allen; to forfeit Allen's bond would have caused hardship on others. He had never tried to influence the courts. The letter to the Beaumont court had been written after their decision had been reached; and as for his letter to the Texas Supreme Court, there was certainly no way that he could have influenced the justices.

It was not his fault that the wrong man had drawn the salary of labor commissioner. Frank Swor had failed to qualify for some reason that Ferguson did not know, but had finally done so recently.

Ferguson and Hanger finished their discussion of the articles of impeachment, with the exception of article 11, late in the afternoon, and Hanger surrendered the governor to M. M. Crane for cross-examination.

There was tension in the Senate chamber as Crane approached the governor, for everyone expected him to begin with the question of the $156,000 loan. Instead, Crane reviewed the entire case, saving the question for last.

Crane first read a *Daily Texan* editorial, which apologized for the article about Ferguson's name being scratched off the ballot by some Austin voters. The paper, said the editorial, had intended no disrespect to the governor. As he had done on so many subjects that incriminated or contradicted him, Ferguson replied to Crane that the editorial "had never been called to his attention."

Crane turned to the matter of the Canyon Normal insurance funds. Yes, Ferguson had withdrawn the money from banks where Governor Colquitt had deposited it, and placed it in the Temple State Bank and the American National Bank of Austin. Forty thousand dollars of it had gone to the Temple State Bank, and it had not drawn interest.

Ferguson hadn't put the money in the state treasury, because if he had, it would have been beyond his control.

"Do you admit that in placing the money in your bank, there was no especial protection for the state and the people?"

"The question of protection never entered my mind."

Ferguson admitted there was an overdraft of his official account when the Canyon Normal account was finally settled. He conceded that $5,600 of the Canyon funds had been used to pay his personal note. But he had not known about it. He had never seen the bank statement which showed the charge. It had been an honest error. Crane was skeptical:

"You were a banker for ten years before you became governor, weren't you, Governor?"

"Yes."

"You looked after all trust funds diligently, didn't you?"

"Yes."

"Well now, while you were in the business of governor, why was it that you let $5,600 of a trust fund get out of that fund and be used for your personal obligation?"

"It appears now that that was done. But was a mistake. I have looked after every cent entrusted to my care."

Crane continued to go over the figures. He showed that the King's Highway funds had been applied to the settlement of the $5,600, and in the meantime, Ferguson had simply owed the money to the state. Ferguson had heard Crane go over this same ground with J. H. Davis, but he could still say little that was convincing. He had not known, he said, that those funds had been applied to the college account.

Ferguson admitted that he owned 300 shares in the Temple State Bank, but denied that the state's deposits produced a profit for him. They were of little consequence. Crane pressed:

"Why did you ask the secretary of state to place his money in the Temple State Bank and to make the deposits as large as possible?"

"I knew it would be advantageous to the bank's statements."

Ferguson did not seem to realize that he was practically admitting his guilt to many of the articles of impeachment. Crane reminded him of his claim yesterday that he had never intended to profit from the deposits in the Temple State Bank.

"Of course I did not. You know, General, I had no idea of profiting. Of course it was some advantage to the bank in having the money. However, that does not mean a profit."

Ferguson may have seen a difference between an advantage and a profit, but it is doubtful that his colleagues in the Texas Senate recognized the distinction, and Crane had again won an important admission. Crane went on to other questions.

In answer, Ferguson denied that he had deposited $60,000 in the Temple State Bank to impress its officers at a time when his overline was being discussed. He admitted that his overline had run to $150,000 but pointed out that other banks loaned overlines. Which banks? For once, Jim Ferguson did not have a ready answer. He could not name the other banks.

Wednesday, September 19—M. M. Crane referred Jim Ferguson to the section of the Texas Constitution that requires all fees received by state officials to be paid at once to the state treasury. Ferguson had never had that particular part of the constitution "called to his attention."

Yes, he was aware that when legislative acts conflicted with the constitution, the constitution prevailed.

Crane read the statute that required fees from outside corporations to be paid to the state treasury; and another statute, which set prison sentences for bank officials who violated the overline limits.

Ferguson protested that the law referred to willful violations and not cases like his, wherein his loans from the Temple State Bank were fully secured and certain to be repaid.

"That is the way you interpret the law?" asked Crane.

"Yes."

"Your construction is that the law can be violated so long as nobody is harmed?"

"Not that. But when a big loan is absolutely secured, there can be no violation of intent."

Crane read the statute that made it illegal to place state money anyplace except the state treasury when the treasury was accessible. Ferguson retorted that there was no guilt unless an attempt at fraud was proven. Anyway, he was being singled out; every other state official who handled state funds made bank deposits. If he was to be impeached, then every official from the Supreme Court down to the head of the University of Texas should be impeached.

But as governor, didn't Ferguson have an obligation to enforce the law, if he knew it was a crime for state officials to place state funds in banks?

Yes, if there was something fraudulent shown.

Did Ferguson think it would be fraudulent if state money was placed in a bank to favor a friend?

Yes.

Or to draw interest?

Yes. If it was done for that purpose, answered Jim Ferguson, then Crane was probably correct. These were astonishing admissions. Given the statutes that Crane had read and the evidence he had introduced, it is difficult to see how Jim Ferguson could continue to maintain that he was completely innocent of any wrongdoing or continue to entertain the idea that he would survive this trial with his position intact. But he did.

Crane continued his assault. In view of the fact that Ferguson had charged the University of Texas professors with corruption for collecting full fare for mileage books, had he done anything to prevent the practice in other state departments?

Any other instances of the practice, said Ferguson, had never been "called to his attention."

Wasn't it true that Ferguson had denied the authority of the legislature to take up impeachment proceedings at this particular session because it had been called for a different purpose, the appropriation for the University of Texas?

"That's true. The denial was in my reply to the bill of impeachment. Whatever may have been my reason for calling the session, I did not intend to surrender my right to any defense I might have."

Crane asked about Professor Battle, the former acting president of the university, and Ferguson's objections to him.

Ferguson explained that he had told Battle that he wanted an itemized budget for the university, in view of the size of the appropriation he was recommending to the legislature. Battle supplied the itemized budget, but it was so voluminous that Ferguson had asked Battle to go over it with him. While they were doing that, Ferguson discovered items for certain posts that the university had no intention of filling. Ferguson objected to "dead men being on the payroll," but on Battle's urging, he finally approved the budget.

Later, though, he found that the budget submitted to the Board of Regents was different: certain items had been omitted and others had been increased — certain salaries, for instance. Ferguson became convinced that Battle had deceived him.

But Crane disputed the governor's claim, reading a letter that Battle had later written to Ferguson, explaining that the changes had been made to save money and that Ferguson had misunderstood certain points during their meeting.

Crane mentioned Ferguson's objection to Dr. Ellis being paid for outside work while drawing a salary from the state. Didn't J. H. Davis look after the governor's private affairs while he was employed by the state?

About twenty minutes a day.

And hadn't Captain Craddock bought cattle for Ferguson in Iowa?

Yes, Craddock had gone to Iowa to investigate cattle disease, and Ferguson had him buy some cattle while he was there.

Ferguson admitted that one of his appointees to the Board of Regents, John Ward, had been his lawyer in Temple, and that another, Dr. MacReynolds, had been the Ferguson family doctor. And he admitted that he had issued warrants for groceries at the mansion, after the courts ruled that he couldn't.

But he denied trying to influence the courts. Judge Brooks of the Beaumont Court of Civil Appeals had asked Ferguson for a letter of recommendation, and Ferguson's letter to the court had been his reply.

"But you sent copies of the letter to other judges of the court. Had they written to you?"

"No," answered Jim Ferguson. "I was just exercising my right to cuss out the court."

Thursday, September 20 — Finally M. M. Crane put the controversial question to Jim Ferguson:

"Governor, there has been evidence adduced, both before the present court and the House Committee of the Whole, that you obtained $156,000, or thereabouts, in cash loans from certain friends this year. Will you please tell us who those friends were?"

Jim Ferguson answered promptly, and even though this

was one of the articles of impeachment against him, he had not changed his mind:

"No. Even if it means losing my office, I will not tell. I mean no disrespect to this court, but my word has gone out. I am bound by a promise."

Crane asked other questions — how many friends? where did they loan him the money? when? — but Ferguson would not answer any of them.

"I believe honestly and candidly," he said, "that I have the constitutional right to decline to furnish this information. My promise has been given not to tell who loaned me this money, and it has not been released, although I have tried to obtain it. I don't believe any court in the land will hold me guilty of contempt."

Now there arose a debate among the senators as to what should be done. One senator called for a report from the rules committee; another wanted the matter referred to the committee on civil jurisprudence. But still another, raising a point of order, maintained that the issue should be decided by the entire Senate. Senator Lattimore obtained the floor and called the motions deliberate attempts by the governor's friends to lead the court away from the main issue.

Lattimore: "The governor only a few minutes ago said he would rather lose his office than divulge the desired information. He is willing to incur the heaviest possible penalty for his silence. What good will it do to refer this matter to a committee for consideration? Suppose the committee should decided to punish for contempt, what will be the effect? The governor has said he will not answer."

The senator had, of course, analyzed the matter perfectly. The Texas Senate was in a quandry, but decided to put the issue to a vote and determined by a margin of 23 to 7 that Jim Ferguson must reveal the names of the friends who had loaned him the money. But Ferguson would not.

Crane asked the governor one last time, and one last time the governor declined to answer. Crane announced that he would pursue the matter no further. He did not want the case "taken down the blind alley of habeus corpus proceedings." He wanted to try the larger question of impeachment. He surrendered Jim Ferguson to his defense counsel, W. A. Hanger, and Hanger promptly asked for a recess until tomorrow.

Friday, September 21 — The members of the High Court of Impeachment reached agreement as to the procedure for final arguments: Jim Ferguson and his assistant counsel, Clarence Martin, would give the closing defense arguments; Will Harris and M. M. Crane would speak for the prosecution. The assistants, Martin and Harris, would argue today, Ferguson and Crane tomorrow.

In his closing argument, Will Harris told the High Court that more was expected of a governor than of a common citizen. The governor of Texas had an obligation to uphold the law. Perhaps Governor Ferguson hadn't intended to profit from the state funds in his bank, but he had hoped they would extend his line of credit. The governor had admitted that the funds had helped his bank "make a showing." Harris challenged the senators to do their duty:

"I know there are many senators who are friends of the governor. It will tear the hearts of these men to vote against him. But I want to tell you now that when it comes down to a decision, these men will do their duty and vote against him."

Clarence Martin responded for Governor Ferguson. The governor had made mistakes, said Martin, but they had been errors of judgment only. There had been no intent to defraud the state, and every cent of the state's money had been repaid. No evidence of an impeachable nature had been introduced; under the constitution, the punishment asked was too great for the offenses alleged.

Saturday, September 22 — At the outset of the session, two of Ferguson's counsel, W. A. Hanger and B. Y. Cummings, denied a newspaper report that they had broken relations with the governor over strategy disagreements. They both maintained that the report was false and malicious, and one of Ferguson's Senate friends promised to have the report investigated.

Whether there was a disagreement over it or not, the defense strategy called for Jim Ferguson to take the stand and deliver the final argument in his own behalf, and that's precisely what he did.

There is no denying that Jim Ferguson was a great orator. In one of his later campaigns for governor, he would hold the podium and deliver a speech even while the Ku Klux Klan was trying to break up his rally, the Klansmen shuffling and stomping their feet then getting up and leaving in unison. That one incident says a great deal about Ferguson's ability as a speaker; it also says something about his tenacity or his stubbornness. His defense speech to the High Court of Impeachment showed both. It lasted for two hours.

"Today, as I appear as the chief actor in this momentous proceeding," said Ferguson, "realizing as I do the solemnity of this occasion, I appreciate the necessity not only of not trying to deceive you, but of not deceiving myself.

"I appreciate as well as you what I am up against. It was apparent that weeks ago there was a certain design on hand. You understand and I understand. There will be interest groups greatly disappointed if you disagree with that plan.

"I know what your verdict will be, but let us not deceive ourselves. Let us dismiss the personal equations involved. Let us forget the influences at work. Decide this case on what has been presented.

"Under the original law, a defendant was given a trial by a jury selected under investigation. If a man expressed bias, he was excluded from service. Had a juror talked about the case, he would have been summoned before the court and probably discharged. Every man has a right to such a trial — except the governor of your state.

"There has been considerable discussion as to whether this is a criminial or a civil case. But what did the senator from Tarrant do this morning? He presented to you a rule that when voting begins, each senator will rise and say 'guilty' or 'not guilty.' Why was it necessary to do that? The court might have voted 'aye' or 'nay.' I am being tried as a criminal, but I defy Mr. Crane, when he has his say, to put his finger on a single act of mine that could be designated a crime.''

The gallery of the Texas Senate was silent, save for the swish of hand fans, as Jim Ferguson orated in the summer heat.

''And let me say right now I am not going to appeal to passion or prejudice or sympathy. I will appeal only to the law of justice, the law of God. They say I have been guilty of this and guilty of that. Let us see what the constitution says.'' He read the portion of the Texas Constitution that says impeachments must be made on neglect of duty, oppression in office, incompetency, or drunkeness.

''There isn't a thing in the articles that can impeach me. Divert yourself of the passion and prejudice, of the influences that have been brought to bear, and this case wouldn't last five minutes.''

This would be one of Ferguson's points always, that he was the victim of ''passion'' and ''madness'' while he defended himself with facts and truth.

''I realize that if I am to be cleared of the charges against me, I must appeal to the hearts and conscience of the senators, so that they will put their hands on their hearts and say in all conscience what they honestly believe.''

Not a single charge against him was an impeachable offense, he claimed; instead the charges were piled up against him like sticks of wood. ''You cannot convict me on generalities. You must deal with certainties.'' And he started back over the charges, bringing up the Canyon City Normal College insurance settlement funds.

''No violation of the law is charged, and none can be shown. If any intent to steal the state's money can be shown in that matter, I release you all to vote me guilty, even those who are my friends.

''When a man goes out to embezzle, he considers whether he can escape detection. Who can think that in the circumstances, any intent on my part can be shown? I had a receipt back of me and a contract to fill in front of me.

''The fact that the fifty-six-hundred-dollar debit in my official account was charged to my personal note openly and aboveboard shows that there was only an error.

"They have charged me with using the Canyon City Normal insurance money to profit myself, but let me call your attention to the fact that I wrote the Temple bank not to increase its loans on the strength of this deposit.

"They complain about my not stopping state offices from depositing state funds in the Temple State Bank. In the same breath almost they abuse me for attempting to stop certain practices at the university. That shows the unreasonableness of the situation.

"It's a great crime to put money in a Temple bank, but let me say that if that money had been put in an Austin bank, this trouble would not have resulted. The university has kept its funds in banks for years, but nobody has tried to impeach its officials.

"And yet some of you are going to impeach me on this proposition. You have not got nerve enough, you're not fair enough, to stand up and vote that what is fish for one shall be fowl for another.

"That brings me to the big question — the university. It was the lust of the university for gold, the unholy spree of the educated hierarchy out there at the university, that precipitated the trouble. They wanted their appropriations — appropriations extravagant but not to be questioned — and the only way they could get them was through impeachment.

"I have been a friend of higher and of all education. My record shows it. My undoing began when I declared for the little schoolhouse along the country road, when I proposed a bill for the expenditure of two million dollars on the rural school.

"George Petty, the president of the Students Association, spilled the beans when he said in a speech that the trouble began with the governor's campaign for the rural school bill. They'd give fifty-thousand dollars if they could recall that statement.

"When I came up here, standing for higher education, the university was for me. But when I attempted to start some reforms out there, they turned against me. That's why I'm here, like Daniel in the Lions' Den, fighting for my life.

"They said to me yesterday, 'If you'll resign, we can look after you.' But let me tell you, I'd rather be impeached a thousand times than to resign.

"This is a fight between the common people and the privileged few, between democracy and autocracy. It is between the little country schoolhouse and the great university on the hill.

"They thought out there they could intimidate me, and they sent a mob down to try it. But they couldn't. I declare solemnly that I set a precedent of great value. If I had yielded, every governor for forty years would have been subjected to the same process of intimidation.

"You've got to get on one side or the other. I didn't start the fight with the university. They started it with me. You rave about the twenty-four-hundred dollars spent at the mansion, but say nothing about the millions laid out at the university. You forget the constitution in one place, but you remember it in another. I don't forget it. I recall the issue, and I put it on you like a mud plaster.

"They talk about the hundred-and-fifty-six-thousand dollars in currency I borrowed. If you let your prejudice control you in that matter, if you vent your spleen, I can't help it. But that was my private business. I have sworn there was nothing wrong about it.

"I started out as a poor boy, a dishwasher at twenty dollars a month. It looks like I am going to be a poor man again, and all because I was trying to save the small fortune I had accumulated.

"I was pressed financially, and I had to seek help. I gave my promise not to tell who helped me, and it is sought to impeach me because I kept my word. The record of a public officer is the service he renders. If it is good, you have no right to inquire into a man's personal life. If I had told about this money and saved my office, there could have been no satisfaction in it for me, because my word would have been broken.

"Now I must close and give way to the official speaker of the investigation.

"When a man has the habit of prosecuting, he's apt to become a persecutor. When Mr. Crane begins to tell you about my faults and my mistakes, I want you to remember that I've done some good things while I've been in office. I've remembered the poor boys and the poor girls, and I've worked to help them.''

Thus Jim Ferguson finished his remarkable speech, just before 11:00 a.m. If he had glossed over certain facts and failed to deal with others, if the speech had been self-serving and rhetorical and even contradictory, it was nevertheless an emotional performance. No one could accuse Farmer Jim of being a quitter. The court adjourned for a noon recess; afterward, M. M. Crane presented the closing argument for the prosecution.

Jim Ferguson had challenged Crane, when he had his say, to point his finger at a single act of Ferguson's that could be designated a crime. Crane was ready to accept the challenge.

Crane proclaimed that it wasn't necessary for impeachment to be brought on charges of statutory offense, but in this case it could be proven that the governor had not only been guilty of acts that ''were not in keeping with his high office'' but had actually violated the criminal statutes. He discussed Ferguson's handling of the Canyon City Normal College insurance funds.

''The governor cannot escape the conclusion, and he ought to admit the truth of it, that that money went into the Temple bank for his profit and that of his friends.

''If it is true that the fifty-six-hundred dollars applied to his personal note from the people's money August 23, 1915, was mistakenly applied, then I say he should be impeached for his failure to properly look after the funds committed to his care.

''He says he learned nothing of the mistake until July of this year, when he found out through the Travis County Grand Jury. My God, Senators! Since when must a governor of Texas find out about his mistakes through a grand jury?

''Think of former governors — Coke, Roberts, Ireland, and Ross — cherished in memory. If they had acted as collection agents for a bank in which they were interested, and gathered state money for deposit in that bank, do you think they would be honored as they are today throughout the confines of this great state?

"The governor says a rich man could take a hundred-thousand dollars from a bank if his security was good and it would be alright. But a stenographer or clerk who would take out a hundred-thousand dollars and later be unable to return it would be guilty of an offense.

"I say he has not learned the first principles of Americanism and democracy. The law of our land is not that kind of law."

The High Court of Impeachment had decided to vote "aye" and "no" instead of "guilty" or "not guilty" to which Ferguson had objected. And now that Crane had finished his final argument, it was time for the vote to be taken. A two-thirds majority was required to pass an article of impeachment; if any one article passed, Jim Ferguson would be removed from office.

The first article — that Ferguson had used Canyon City Normal College insurance funds to settle a personal obligation — was read and the vote taken. The article passed, with 27 ayes and 4 noes.

Thus Jim Ferguson was convicted; the office of governor was no longer his, and Will Hobby was now governor of Texas, rather than acting governor. At least all of this seemed to be true, but in fact some startling events were yet to occur.

Ferguson left the Senate chamber after the first vote went against him, but he returned to hear some of the later votes, and he joined in the laughter that erupted on the third vote, when his old friend, Senator Clark, announced that he was voting no and intended to vote no on all 21 charges.

The High Court passed 10 of the articles of impeachment and rejected 11. In addition to the first, these are the other articles that were sustained:

2.   That Ferguson had kept the proceeds of the Canyon City Normal College insurance settlement in the Temple State Bank for more than a year without interest, the deposit working to Ferguson's profit — 26 ayes; 5 noes.

6.   That he had deposited $60,000 of the state's money

in the same bank and profited from this deposit as well — 24 ayes; 7 noes.

7. That he had assisted in the deposit of another $250,000 in state funds to the credit of the Temple State Bank, again to his own profit — 26 ayes; 5 noes.

11. That he had refused to reveal who had loaned him $156,000, his refusal being an act of offical misconduct — 27 ayes; 4 noes.

12. That he had diverted funds from the state adjutant general to payment on the Canyon City Normal College — 27 ayes; 4 noes.

14. That he had induced the officers of the Temple State Bank to lend him money in excess of the legal limit, even while he was sworn to enforce the law — 26 ayes; 5 noes.

16. That he had sought to influence the Board of Regents of the Univesity of Texas to do his autocratic will — 22 ayes; 9 noes.

17. That he had sought to violate the law by removing regents of the University of Texas without good cause — 22 ayes; 8 noes; 1 not voting.

19. That he had sought to influence the chairman of the Board of Regents, Wilbur P. Allen, by remitting a $5,000 bail bond to him — 21 ayes; 10 noes.

With the passage of these 10 articles, the impeachment trial was over, and the Ferguson episode should have ended. But there was still the matter of a judgment to be rendered by the High Court. Under the Texas Constitution, the Senate might bar Ferguson from further office in addition to removing him from office now, and that matter had to be decided. While the Senate was grappling with this issue, Jim Ferguson would try to keep his political future alive by resigning from office. He had said that he would rather be impeached a thousand times than to resign, but he apparently hadn't considered the possibility that the Senate would bar him from holding any office again.

Ferguson would later make much of the fact that the legislature had accused him of more things than even the Senate itself would agree to, and it is interesting to consider the articles of impeachment that were rejected. Some of the rejected articles received a majority of the votes in favor, but failed to obtain the

F. O. FULLER, the speaker of the Texas House of Representatives, issued a call for a special session of the legislature to consider impeaching Governor Ferguson, despite the fact that only the governor of Texas has the authority to call a special session. Fuller introduced the charges against Ferguson, including a startling allegation that Ferguson had tried to bribe him.

— *Photo from Texas State Library*

necessary two-thirds margin. These articles failed:

3.   That two notes of $37,500 each had been transferred from the Temple State Bank to the Houston National Exchange Bank to cover up Governor Ferguson's obligations to the Temple State Bank — 18 ayes; 13 noes.

4.   That Ferguson had attempted to deceive the legislature by stating at the March investigation that he had paid $127,500 in cash on his debts to the Temple State Bank, when in fact he paid $75,000 of the sum with two notes on which he himself was guarantor — 18 ayes; 13 noes.

5.   That he had testified in March that he was not indebted to the Temple State Bank, when in fact he owned the bank a note for $11,200 — 14 ayes; 17 noes.

8.   That he had sought to have funds of the Texas Highway Commission deposited in the Temple State Bank in order to profit from them — 7 ayes; 22 noes.

9.   That he had deposited state funds in the Temple State Bank and other banks when the state treasury was open to receive them — 15 ayes; 12 noes; 4 not voting.

10.   That he had testified in March that he owed the Temple State Bank nothing, when in fact he owed it more than the law allowed — 13 ayes; 18 noes.

13.   That he had failed to refund the money that he had spent for groceries and other items at the governor's mansion — 15 ayes; 16 noes.

15.   That he had sought to set aside the Texas Constitution by vetoeing the appropriation for the University of Texas — 6 ayes; 24 noes; 1 not voting.

18.   That he had libeled the members of the faculty of the University of Texas by calling them liars and grafters without proving his charges or prosecuting the faculty members — 9 ayes; 20 noes; 2 not voting.

20.   That he had sought to influence the courts in matters in which he had a personal interest — 15 ayes; 16 noes.

21.   That he had permitted C. W. Woodman to continue as state labor commissioner after the Senate had refused to confirm him — 2 ayes; 29 noes.

After the final vote had been taken, Ferguson was surrounded by friends and well-wishers. The now ex-governor maintained his composure and even tried to reassure his friends. "Everything will be alright," he told them.

For the business of drafting a formal judgment, the High Court assigned the matter to the committee on civil jurisprudence, which would meet Monday. Meanwhile, Saturday night, Ferguson issued a statement to the press:

> The loyalty of my friends more than overbalances any reaction that I might have at the action of the Senate. No man ever had better friends, and I am proud to give this expression of my appreciation of their unequaled loyalty.

Ferguson no doubt intended his deepest thanks for the four senators who had voted him innocent on all 21 charges — Senators Clark, Hall, Parr and Woodward.

Ferguson also had friends on the committee on civil jurisprudence, and on Monday his friends pressed for leniency for the impeached governor; they supported a minority report that proposed to simply remove Jim Ferguson from office. The majority report would remove him and also disqualify him from further office.

On Tuesday, September 25, the Senate met again to adopt the final judgment and debated the two reports. It soon became apparent that the majority report would be adopted and that Ferguson would be barred from further office. Ferguson's friends fought though.

One senator pleaded that Jim Ferguson should not be placed in a class all alone, where no pardoning power on earth could reprove him. A final judgment should be reserved for the people, so that Jim Ferguson could at least run for office again.

Ferguson's friends tried to soften the impact of the judgment with various amendments, but they all failed. One amendment would have limited Ferguson's disqualification to five years; another took the form of a proviso that a future legislature could restore his right to hold office. The latter amendment failed after two points of order were raised — one, that a current legislature couldn't instruct a later one, and second, that the judgment of the High Court of Impeachment was final and could not be reopened. Finally, at 5:25 p.m., the Senate adopted the majority report by a vote of 25 to 3. The judgment was now formal and final:

> It is adjudged by the Senate of the state of Texas, sitting at their chamber in the city of Austin, that the said James E. Ferguson be and is hereby removed from office and is disqualified to hold any office of honor, trust or profit under the state of Texas.

But hearing of the way the debate was going in the Senate, Jim Ferguson decided to offer a last-moment resignation. He wrote a letter resigning the office of governor and managed to hand the document to the secretary of state before the Senate took its final vote on the judgment. So that now one legal question would remain: Had Jim Ferguson been impeached, or had he resigned?

Although he resigned — supposedly — just a short while before the judgment of the Senate was rendered on Tuesday, Ferguson dated his document with Monday's date, September 24:

> To Hon. Churchill J. Bartlett, Secretary of State of Texas, Austin, Texas:
>
> In order that I may have sufficient time and proper opportunity to present the merits of my candidacy for the office of governor for a third term, and in order that there may be no interference with the right of the people to elect me to that office, which belongs to the people, I hereby tender this, my resignation as governor of Texas, same to take effect immediately. I take this action only because I have been reliably informed that the Senate of the state of Texas is attempting to pass some pretended and illegal order or judgment for the purpose of preventing the people of Texas from electing me governor for a third time and to prevent my holding said office by virture of their election.
>
> Witness my hand this, the twenty-fourth day of September, 1917. — (Signed) James E. Ferguson.

Ferguson explained to reporters that the fact that the Senate had convicted him on only 10 charges proved that "in their madness to impeach him they had made more untrue charges than they themselves would say were true." And now, he claimed, they didn't want the people to be able to pass judgment on their judgment of him. For the time being, autocracy had trampled democracy. But the people would rise up; they would have a chance to rule on this. Jim Ferguson was leaving Austin, but he would be back.

The next day, two senators, angered by Ferguson's remarks, including his statement to the press that he had not been given the same fair trial that would have been afforded to a "nigger crapshooter," read statements into the record that they had been wrong to vote against disqualification.

Three days later, on Saturday, September 29, the Texas legislature adjourned, and on the same day the *Temple Daily Telegram* carried a brief epitaph to the entire affair:

> Ex-governor Ferguson and his family arrived in Temple yesterday, from Austin, coming overland in an automobile.

Jim Ferguson soon dropped from the news in the *Temple Daily Telegram* altogether. There was a war on, and the people in Temple had other things to worry about, like the price of cotton, which had dropped.

Trainloads of recruits had been passing through town enroute to the training station at Camp Travis. Their trains were decorated with streamers like "To Hell With the Kaiser" and "We're the Best Bunch in Texas." The Red Cross set up refreshment centers for the recruits in Temple and in Belton. One night in Belton a parade was held for the Bell County men leaving on the midnight train for Camp Travis.

Later in the fall, boxing champion Jess Williard came to town with a Wild West Show. By then, Jim Ferguson had become another ordinary Temple citizen. In Austin, Will Hobby was governor of Texas.

5

The Acting Governor

Will Hobby, born the son of a lawyer in Moscow, Texas, in 1878, was first and last a newspaperman. His family moved to Houston when he was a boy, and when he was 16, he quit school and went to work for the *Houston Post* as a clerk. While working at that job, he had a very minor brush with history: He directed the deputy who was carrying process papers to William Sidney Porter — alias O. Henry — who was working as a writer for the *Post*. Porter was supposed to go to Austin and answer questions about some missing bank funds; instead, he fled to Honduras.

Hobby became a reporter when he was 22, and by the time he was 26, he had been made the managing editor of the *Post*. He later left that paper to join the *Beaumont Enterprise,* where he became, by age 35, publisher and part owner. In Beaumont, he was active in civic affairs and local democratic politics. In 1914, at the age of 36, on the urging of friends, he entered the race for lieutenant governor of Texas. Running on a platform similar to Jim Ferguson's, he was elected.

The lieutenant governorship was a prestigious but somewhat ceremonial post. The lieutenant governor presided over the Senate and received the same salary as a senator — five dollars a day while the legislature was in session.

Hobby continued his journalism career while serving as lieutenant governor and was elected president of the Texas Associated Press Managing Editors Association. He also pressed for and won the establishment of the Texas Election Bureau, an agency that collected election returns from the state's various newspapers by telephone and tabulated the totals. As governor, his proudest

WILL HOBBY, a newspaperman from Beaumont, was elected lieutenant governor of Texas in 1914. When the Texas House of Representatives impeached Jim Ferguson, Hobby became acting governor, and after Ferguson's conviction, governor. He won a second term in his own right in 1918, and set a remarkable record as a great wartime governor. After that term, he retired from politics and devoted the rest of his life to journalism.

— Photo from Texas State Library

achievement was a bill he pushed through the Texas legislature, a law that protected reporters from libel suits in matters concerning court proceedings, public meetings, etcetera. But in fact that law was only one of Will Hobby's minor accomplishments as a political leader.

On August 24, 1917, after the Texas House of Representatives had adopted articles of impeachment against Jim Ferguson, Lieutenant Governor Will Hobby, accompanied by his brother and brother-in-law, went to the executive offices in the state capitol, conferred with Jim Ferguson, and took over the duties of governor.

It is fair to say that from his first day as acting governor Hobby conducted himself with grace, diplomacy and assurance. His first act was to invite Jim Ferguson to keep his headquarters in the governor's office until the matter was settled one way or the other, an invitation that Ferguson accepted.

And since the special session of the legislature would expire at the end of the month, Hobby had to issue a call for another special session, and in so doing, he immediately began to distance himself from Ferguson and the impeachment affair, for he called the session officially to deal with five matters: 1. To deal with the pink bollworm blight that threatened the Texas cotton crop. 2. To protect men called into service from civil suits filed after their enlistment. 3. To protect the rights of soldiers in property matters. 4. To provide legislation for drought relief. 5. Only last did he call for the fair and impartial trial of Governor Jim Ferguson.

The legislature that impeached Ferguson also acted on the other proposals of the acting governor. Laws protecting the rights of soldiers were enacted, and Hobby himself arranged for state funds to be deposited in banks in the counties most affected by the drought; he also quarantined the cotton in the counties where the pink bollworm blight was most severe. And, of course, he signed the appropriation for the University of Texas.

He also scored legislative victories in the next session of the legislature, in 1918. One measure he recommended, and one which passed, gave women the right to vote in the Democratic primary of 1918.

Hobby stood for re-election that year, and his opponent in the Democratic primary was none other than Farmer Jim Ferguson himself. Ferguson had vowed to return to office, and was taking the earliest opportunity to do so.

Hobby's friends urged him to keep Ferguson's name out of the primary ballot, citing the judgment of the High Court of Impeachment, but he refused. Instead, he whipped Ferguson soundly in the primary. Hobby set a precedent for Texas politicians in that campaign by revealing the sources and uses of all his campaign funds.

There has been no adequate assessment of the women's vote in the primary election, but Ferguson had argued against women's suffrage at the Democratic National Convention of 1916, and since Hobby had just engineered passage of the right of women to vote in this particular election, it is safe to assume that most of the female vote went to Hobby.

After winning the election, Hobby was finally sworn in as governor in his own right, thereby correcting one point on which the men who conducted the Ferguson impeachment had failed to follow the Texas Constitution: the constitution requires that the governor take an oath of office, but after Ferguson was convicted, no one thought to swear in Will Hobby.

In April, 1918, President Woodrow Wilson called on Texas to provide more cavalry for the Great War, and Hobby ordered the organization of two additional Texas brigades. That spring, he appointed a military welfare committee with himself as chairman, and led campaigns for the maximum protection of food and the sale of liberty bonds.

In October, 1918, the influenza epidemic spread to Texas and ultimately afflicted most of the soldiers stationed at Texas military camps. (Texas was the main training area for American troops during the First World War; 250,000 men were trained in the state.) Over 9,000 men died in Army camps during October, and Hobby persuaded the national draft director, General Crowder, to suspend that month's draft to avoid sending new men to the contaminated camps. In November, Hobby was himself stricken with influenza, but left his sick bed to attend memorial services for Austin men who had been killed in the war.

Later, he designated a special day for Texans to gather materials for gas masks, and in 1919 he pressed for a law that permitted returning soldiers to use their discharge papers in lieu of poll tax receipts in order to vote.

If there was tragedy in the governorship of Jim Ferguson, it was this: While Jim Ferguson was waging a petty, personal war against the University of Texas, he was squandering time and energy that should have been spent on the real war and the drought and the cotton blight. It fell to Will Hobby to serve out the term to which Ferguson had been elected, and Hobby left an impeccable record as a great wartime governor.

During Hobby's second term, a boundary dispute between Oklahoma and Texas arose, after oil had been discovered beneath the bed of the Red River, near the southern bank. The Red River is the dividing line between the two states, but Oklahoma claimed that the southern bank of the Red was the boundary, while Texas maintained that the boundary was the middle of the River.

Texas was represented in the legal proceedings by the state's attorney general, but Will Hobby called a special session of the legislature to determine Texas' position and course of action on the matter. The issue was finally decided by the U.S. Supreme Court, which awarded the oil to neither Oklahoma or Texas: Instead, the court assigned the oil to the United States, as trustee for the Indian tribes who lived in Oklahoma.

In 1920, the pink bollworm blight had grown worse, and the federal government proposed to quarantine all Texas cotton, but Hobby went to Washington and persuaded administration officials to delay the action. With the help of scientists from Texas A. and M. University, the blight was finally eradicated.

Also in 1920, the island city of Galveston was paralyzed by a longshoremen's strike, and violence erupted. Ultimately a state of virtual anarchy enveloped the city.

In June, Governor Hobby declared martial law in Galveston and dispatched the Texas National Guard under General Jacob Wolters to restore order to the city. Wolters and his troops had difficulty in doing that, and in July, Hobby suspended the city's officials, including the city judge and police, and gave Wolters full control of the police, the jails, and the city court.

He maintained martial law in Galveston for the rest of the summer and didn't return the city to local control until order had been restored and a group of the city's officials petitioned him to do so. He withdrew martial law on September 30, but appointed a Texas Ranger to continue to supervise Galveston's law enforcement officers.

When his full term as governor expired, Hobby retired from Texas politics and returned to journalism, first in Beaumont but later back with the *Houston Post*. He eventually became owner and publisher of the paper. Hobby's standing with the Texas voters was so high that he could certainly have been reelected governor had he wished, or he could have easily won election to the U.S. Senate. But he was a newspaperman.

In 1952, Hobby made television campaign appearances for Dwight D. Eisenhower. His second wife, Oveta Culp Hobby, whom he married in 1931, served as director of the Women's Army Corps during the Second World War, and also served in Eisenhower's cabinet as Secretary of Health, Education and Welfare.

In 1982, Hobby's son, Will Hobby, Jr., was reelected lieutenant governor of Texas.

6

Jim Ferguson and the Ku Klux Klan

Jim Ferguson returned home to Temple after his impeachment, but his political career was far from over. He would run for office again and again, and if he ever vindicated himself, then he did so in the Texas gubernatorial election of 1924, when he ran against and beat the Ku Klux Klan. But first, to consider a few unresolved matters:

After Jim Ferguson left Austin, the Travis County district attorney quashed the criminal charges against Jim Ferguson for what he termed "lack of evidence." And Board of Regents of the University of Texas re-hired the professors whom Ferguson had caused to be fired, with the exception of one.

The school secretary, John A. Lomax, had left Texas, and would continue his career as a folklorist and folk song collector. In 1910, Lomax had already published a book of old folk songs called *Songs of the Cowboys,* which published for the first time such western ballads as "Git Along, Little Dogies" and "The Old Chisholm Trail."

Collecting and recording songs in penitentiaries throughout the South, he would discover the great black folk singer known as Leadbelly and publish a book of Negro folk songs. Lomax and his son Alan later collaborated on other collections, and John Lomax is considered a pioneer in the field of collecting folk songs, and perhaps its preeminent practitioner.

In 1918, Ferguson attempted to keep his promise and return to office for a third term as governor, but he lost the primary election to Will Hobby. Hobby had won the confidence of the Texas voters, and Ferguson's case was lost from the outset.

KU KLUX KLAN ceremonies like the one seen here were common in Texas in the early 20s, until Miriam Ferguson signed the 1924 anti-mask law. Even while the Fergusons were campaigning against the Klan in 1924, the KKK held a nighttime induction ceremony in the Midway Park in Temple.

— *Austin-Travis County Collection*

It was a bitter campaign. Ferguson at one point made the regrettable comment that Hobby was a man "on whom the Almighty failed to endow the normal attributes that go to make up a man."

Listeners assumed that Ferguson was referring to Hobby's short stature and prominent ears (although Hobby was not an unattractive man).

Hobby responded in a speech that although Ferguson might not approve of his attributes, "at least the Almighty gave me the sense to know the difference between my own money and money that belongs to the state."

Ferguson's secret loan was an issue, with Hobby challenging the ex-governor to finally tell who had loaned him the $156,000. Ferguson declined to tell, and Hobby won the election. Later, though, an Internal Revenue Service audit revealed that the Texas Brewers Association had given the money to Ferguson on a friendly basis.

L. A. Adoue, a former president of the Galveston Brewing Company, claimed that the brewers had been afraid that the loan would be misunderstood and used by prohibitionists, and so obtained Ferguson's promise of secrecy. So, of course, Ferguson's claim to the High Court of Impeachment that no one seeking legislation had loaned him the money was false. In his first term, he had vetoed a bill calling for another referendum on prohibition.

After his defeat, Ferguson published a sporadic newspaper in Temple, calling it the *Ferguson Forum* and using it to discuss his political views. He devoted the rest of his time to ranching.

In 1920, he ran for President of the United States — or so he claimed — on his own one-man American Party ticket; he got 60,000 votes, all of them in Texas.

In 1922, he ran for the U.S. Senate, and did well enough to face Earl B. Mayfield, the candidate of the Ku Klux Klan, in a primary run-off election. Ferguson campaigned vigorously, as he always did, promising to "take the courts out of the swamps and put them back in the courthouses." But Mayfield won the run-off, and in November was elected to the Senate.

The Ku Klux Klan arrived in Texas in 1920, when its founder, William Joseph Simmons, visited Houston during a reunion of Texas Confederate Civil War veterans. While he was in Houston, Simmons inducted a number of Kleagles (recruiters) into the Invisible Empire, and empowered them to establish the Klan in Texas. By the end of 1921, the Kleagles had inducted 80,000 Texans into the Invisible Empire of Ku Klux Klan.

From 1920 to 1922, Texas Klansmen sought to enforce Protestant ethics and moral standards in communities throughout the state by holding kangaroo courts, beating infidels and adulterers, and terrorizing black people. There were innumerable acts of violence, including some murders, attributed to masked Klansmen, but precious few prosecutions.

But in 1922 the Klan attempted to downplay its vigilante role in favor of entering mainstream politics. This was the case not only in Texas but throughout the Union.

The new tactic was inspired mostly by a Klansman named Hiram Wesley Evans. Evans had been the Exalted Cyclops of Dallas Klan 66, but in 1922, he had advanced to Imperial Kliggrapp (national secretary), and it was from this post that he directed the Klan's foray into politics.

Three Klansmen entered the 1922 Texas senatorial primary on the Democratic ticket, but Evans wanted the Klan to endorse just one of them so that the Klan vote wouldn't be divided. He therefore gave the endorsement to his favorite, Earl B. Mayfield. But individual Klansmen objected to the move, condemning it as an abuse of power, and finally Evans agreed for the matter to be put to a vote.

Hence, there was a preliminary primary election in 1922 for the Ku Klux Klansmen only. Mayfield won the straw vote of the Realm of Texas and entered the Democratic primary with the exclusive endorsement of the Klan, and after defeating Jim Ferguson in a run-off, as we have seen, he was elected to the U.S. Senate.

In November of 1922, Evans consolidated his power in the Invisible Empire. Capitalizing on the feeling of many Klansmen that founder and Imperial Grand Wizard Simmons was more interested in collecting dues and getting rich than he was in advancing the goals of the Klan, Evans led a revolt against Simmons.

At the Imperial Klonvocation of 1922 (national convention), Evans displaced Simmons as Imperial Grand Wizard, with Simmons being given the empty title of Emperor.

The year 1922 was the best year the Ku Klux Klan had in politics. In Texas the Klan elected a senator and gained control of the city governments of Dallas, Fort Worth, and Wichita Falls; elsewhere, it elected governors in Georgia and Oregon.

By 1924, Evans presided over a Klan that claimed five million members nationwide, and he set it as one of his top priorities to elect a Ku Klux Klan governor of Texas. Evans gave his backing to Felix D. Robertson, a judge, a prohibitionist, and the grandson of a Confederate general. Another straw vote was held, and once again the Klan approved Evans' selection. With a unified effort, the Ku Klux Klan stood an excellent chance of electing a governor of Texas; for the state was said to have 400,000 members of the Invisible Empire.

But by 1924, many people had become bitterly opposed to the Ku Klux Klan, and one of the candidates for governor of Texas was Farmer Jim Ferguson. Like other events in politics, the Ku Klux Klan made for strange bedfellows and strange enemies. In Fort Worth, Ferguson's old defense counsel, W. A. Hanger, was serving as a Kleagle for the Invisible Empire. In Dallas, a Citizens League had organized to oppose the Klan; the head of the Citizens League was the distinguished and aged attorney, M. M. Crane.

In March of 1924, Jim Ferguson declared his candidacy once again for governor of Texas and published a lengthy platform in the *Temple Daily Telegram*, calling for tax cuts and less government spending. Ferguson was beginning to show his age more now — his hair was turning white and thinning out, and he had grown heavier around the middle — but he could still draw a crowd.

In May, however, a private citizen named John Maddox filed a suit to prevent Ferguson's name from being printed on the Democratic primary ballot on grounds that it was prohibited by the judgment of the High Court of Impeachment. On May 15, the case of Ferguson vs. Maddox came before the 55th District Court in Houston.

Attorneys in the case, including Ferguson's lawyer, W. G. Love, whom Ferguson had once appointed to the Board of Regents of the University of Texas, met and drew up an agreed-to statement of facts. This was done to avoid a prolonged review of the impeachment of 1917.

On May 17, the court granted the injunction Maddox had sought and restrained the Democratic executive committee from printing Ferguson's name on the ballot. W. G. Love promptly appealed the decision, but on May 28, the Court of Appeals upheld the injunction.

The next day, Jim Ferguson's wife, Miriam Amanda Ferguson, filed her application with the Democratic executive committee as a candidate for governor of Texas. And W. G. Love appealed Jim Ferguson's case to the Texas Supreme Court.

Love submitted certified questions of law to the court, attacking the injunction on several grounds: that the constitution did not define an impeachable offense; that the legislature which impeached Ferguson had not been called into special session for that purpose; that Ferguson had been impeached during one session of the legislature and tried during another; and that the Texas Senate could not legally have impeached him anyway, as he was a private citizen at the time, having already resigned the office of governor.

On June 2, two of the justices of the Texas Supreme Court disqualified themselves from the case. One had been a senator during Ferguson's trial, and the other had served in the attorney general's office, which had given opinions on points of law to the Senate during the impeachment trial. The next day, two judges were appointed to sit as special justices on the case, and on June 4, deliberations began. On June 12, the court rendered its ruling: it upheld the decision of the Court of Appeals and rejected each of Love's arguments.

As far as the legislature impeaching Ferguson during a special session called for a different purpose, the court decided, "The powers of the House and Senate in relation to impeachment exist at all times."

The decision dismissed the notion that Ferguson had already resigned the office: "On no admissable theory could this resignation impair the jurisdiction or power of the court to render its judgment. The subject matter was within its jurisdiction. It had jurisdiction of the person of the governor; it had heard the evidence and declared him guilty . . . The purpose of the constitutional provision may not be thwarted by an eleventh-hour resignation."

The court also ruled that although the constitution did not specifically define impeachable offenses, they were clearly designated by the term "impeachment."

And the Texas Supreme Court had a very high estimation of the powers of the High Court of Impeachment:

"The Senate sitting in an impeachment trial is just as truly a court as is this court. Its jurisdiction is very limited, but such as it has is of the highest. It is original, exclusive, and final. Within the scope of its constitutional authority, no one may gainsay its judgment."

And so now, seven years after the verdict of the High Court of Impeachment, its judgment was finally upheld. Jim Ferguson's name would not appear on the ballot as a candidate for governor.

But even while the court had been deliberating, Ferguson's wife, Miriam, had been certified as a candidate, and two days after the court's ruling, Ferguson and his wife appeared together at a rally in Copperas Cove, a small town some 30 miles west of Temple.

Ferguson told a crowd of about 2,000 that his wife would represent the Ferguson platform." Mrs. Ferguson gave a brief speech, saying that she would "seek vindication at the hands of the people for the wrongs done her husband, herself, and their children, through the assaults of enemies." Then Jim introduced his tax reduction plan and promised to reduce government spending, and assailed the Ku Klux Klan:

The Ku Klux Klan is either a good thing or a bad thing. If it is a good thing, it ought to be left alone. If it is a bad thing, it ought to be driven out of politics, and made to quit raising so much trouble between friends and neighbors, and members of the same family.

The only way to do this is to turn on the light of pitiless publicity. For that reason, I have proposed the two laws, requiring members of all secret organizations to be filed in the county clerk's office — and the drastic penalty of a penitentiary term for people caught in public or private with masks on.

It is said that because Miriam Amanda Ferguson's initials were M. A., she became known as Ma Ferguson. Whether that is true or not, the bumper stickers in Texas in 1924 said "Me for Ma" and "Pa aint bad either." So Jim Ferguson and his wife, Miriam, would finish their careers, or their joint career in Texas politics as "Ma and Pa" Ferguson. It is the way they are still remembered by older people in Texas.

There were several candidates for the Democratic nomination for governor of Texas in 1924, including a former lieutenant governor, Lynch Davidson, but in the end, it came down to a contest between Felix D. Robertson of the Ku Klux Klan and Ma Ferguson of Temple.

The primary was to be held on July 26. On June 17, Mrs. Ferguson announced that since she was new to politics, she would not give any long speeches. She would accompany Jim on campaign trips, and she would trust in Providence to guide her. Her one ambition was to clear her family name of the "awful judgment."

The summer of 1924 was a long, hot one. On July 5, Ku Klux Klansmen in Long Beach, New Jersey, stoned an effigy of the Catholic Al Smith. On July 7, the Klan gained new strength in Texas: Indeed, 100 new members were initiated into the Klan in a nighttime ceremony in Midway Park in Temple, Texas. There were now said to be about 800 members of the Klan in Jim Ferguson's own hometown.

That same week, Calvin Coolidge's son, Calvin, Jr., died in the White House, and the deadlocked National Democratic Convention reached its 100th ballot in Madison Square Garden. Under strong Klan domination, the Texas delegation was casting its votes under the unit rule for William Gibbs McAdoo. (McAdoo was not a Klansman, but one of the alternatives was Al Smith.) Finally, on July 10, Texas voted with the majority for the compromise slate of James W. Davis and Charles W. Bryan.

In Texas, Felix D. Robertson was campaigning for governor on a platform of "honesty, Christianity and common sense." He downplayed his Klan connection until the primary date drew near, then finally made his position clear. In one speech he succinctly summarized the nefarious philosophy of the Klan:

> I am the man the Ku Klux Klan endorsed, and I am proud of it. I don't care whether it suits the Pope in Rome or not.
>
> I am carrying the banner of white supremacy — against foreign immigration — for the suppression of every foreign language newspaper in the country — against special privileges — and for America for Americans — and the rule of the white man from Washington to the school board.

The primary was held on Saturday, July 26, and it was soon apparent that Felix D. Robertson had won, although not by a majority; he would have to face a runoff election. But as to who had finished second and would enter the runoff with him, the answer was not apparent; it took several days before the results of the election were finally known, the lead for second place seesawing between Lynch Davidson and Miriam Ferguson. Finally, on July 30, the Texas Election Bureau certified Mrs. Ferguson as the second-place candidate, and a runoff was scheduled for August 23.

Almost immediately, reporters beseiged the Ferguson home in Temple. Mrs. Ferguson told them that she would trust in God and would seek the advice of her husband and other patriotic Texans; and bootlegging drugstores, she said, would have to go. As governor, she would insist on it.

On August 6, the Fergusons spoke at a rally in Dallas. Ferguson claimed that the people would "rather have a woman with a good, constructive platform than a man with no platform at all.'' Ferguson was going to reduce taxes and reduce government spending, and only Ferguson ''offered protection against the designs and intentions of the Ku Klux Klan to take away the liberties of the people.''

The next day, the Fergusons were greeted by a crowd of 10,000 in the Cotton Palace Coliseum in Waco. Ma explained that she was not running for governor out of ambition, but out of a desire to clear the Ferguson name for her children and her grandchildren. And Pa lambasted the Ku Klux Klan. If Robertson was elected, said Ferguson, he would ''take the advice and counsel of the 'grand gizzards' of Texas.'' But Jim would see to it that the laws were ''enforced in the courthouses instead of the river bottoms.''

On August 12, Felix Robertson came to Temple to campaign on Ferguson's home ground, and spoke to a crowd of about 5,000 in the city park. He had come to Temple, where everyone knew Ferguson, said Robertson, ''to brand Jim Ferguson an infamous, lowdown liar, and worse than that, he knows he is a liar.''

Robertson discussed Ferguson's impeachment and his secret loan, claiming that just as the brewers had given Ferguson the $156,000, now it was the brewers and the bootleggers who were backing Ferguson for governor.

The next week, Robertson returned to Bell County, addressing a crowd of Great War veterans in Belton, condemning Ferguson's war record — his failure to enlist (as Robertson had), and his failure to buy liberty bonds. The next day, Ferguson responded to Robertson's Belton speech, claiming that he had in fact bought $25,000 in liberty bonds, and naming a banker in Clifton who could verify it. But the banker soon admitted that although Ferguson had contracted to buy the bonds, he had later backed out and paid a $50 cancellation fee.

On the eve of the election, Ferguson confidently predicted that his wife would be elected by a margin of 250,000 votes. Anyone who didn't believe it should ''save this paper for a reference.'' On August 23, Mrs. Ferguson did indeed defeat Felix D. Roberton, by a margin of some 97,000 votes.

Winning the Democratic primary was tantamount to being

elected, but after Mrs. Ferguson's victory, supporters of the University of Texas launched a last ditch campaign to prevent Ferguson's return to Austin by installing a university law professor, George C. Butte, as the Republican candidate for governor. The Republican Party had previously named a different candidate, but that gentleman, T. P. Lee, had sent a telegram to Ferguson, wishing his wife luck in the primary and saying that Lee would then be happy with the usual Republican honor of knowing that state would be well governed. Dr. Butte replaced Mr. Lee as the Republican candidate, but Miriam Ferguson easily won the election.

Although she was a stand-in candidate for her husband, Mrs. Ferguson was not merely a figurehead. She did not, for instance, remain at home in the governor's mansion while her husband conducted the business of the office. Mrs. Ferguson spent her time in the governor's office and maintained a staff and had a voice in the affairs of the state of Texas. Her reign as governor was actually a joint governorship, conducted by herself and her husband.

In 1925, she appointed three women to sit briefly as special justices on the Texas Supreme Court. It may be the only all-woman supreme court to ever sit in any state in the Union, and Mrs. Ferguson's campaign manager, Hortense Ward, sat as the chief justice.

Soon after her inauguration, the Texas legislature passed an anti-mask law, imposing a fine of up to $500 and a prison term of up to ten years for "going near public places disguised, entering private houses or churches disguised, committing masked assault, or parading masked." On March 7, 1925, Mrs. Ferguson signed the bill into law.

Jim Ferguson had said that the Ku Klux Klan should be driven out of politics, and the anti-mask law proved to be an effective way of doing it. Texas membership in the Klan soon fell to a pitiful few. The same was true throughout the rest of the Union. Other states passed anti-mask laws, and public opinion turned bitterly against the Invisible Empire.

The anti-mask law, however, could not prevent the Klansmen from holding ceremonies on their own private property, and in 1926, the Ku Klux Klan of the Realm of Texas held its last Klorero (state convention) in the Klan's own park in Temple, Texas. Attendance at the Klorero was sparse; the Klan's attempt to take a final slap at its nemesis, Jim Ferguson, was seen as a dismal failure.

7

Jim Ferguson and Richard Nixon: Constitutional Questions

There are certain curious similarities between the debater from Salado College and the debater from Whittier College. Jim Ferguson and Richard Nixon both grew up under difficult circumstances. Jim Ferguson was reared by his widowed mother, who had to struggle with five children. The family was poor, and Jim had to work. His father's death, when Jim was a little boy, deeply affected him, and he always remembered the funeral and the casket that neighbors built in the Ferguson home.

Richard Nixon's family was also poor, and like Ferguson, Richard had to work from the time he was very young. Nixon was deeply affected by the death of his two brothers from tuberculosis.

Ferguson married when he was 28 years old, Nixon when he was 27. Both men had two daughters, and each became close emotionally to one of his daughters. Nixon was defended by his daughter Julie during the Watergate crisis, and Julie served him as a source of strength and encouragement. She also helped to influence President Gerald Ford to grant a pardon to her father.

During Ferguson's difficult years following his impeachment, his daughter Ouida helped him, campaigned with him, and lent him money. It was Ouida who wrote the biography which euologizes Farmer Jim.

Ferguson and Nixon both became lawyers, both attained high office, and both were impeached. (Granted that Nixon's impeachment was not completed.) Both men sank into periods of oblivion and exile during their lifetime, and both made incredible comebacks.

Nixon had lost a presidential election to John Kennedy and a California gubernatorial election to Pat Brown in 1962, when he came back six years later to gain the presidency. (The television commentator Howard K. Smith delivered a "Political Obituary of Richard Nixon" in 1962, and Nixon was thought to be dead politically.)

Ferguson had been impeached as governor and had lost three successive elections, and was practically broke financially, when he whipped the Ku Klux Klan and his wife was elected governor. Nixon was 55 when he won in 1968; Ferguson was 51 when he won in 1924.

Both men had obsessive interests in making money and were plagued by financial difficulties. Even as early as 1952, Richard Nixon was accused of financial misconduct because of a secret campaign fund. (The accusations resulted in Nixon's celebrated "Checkers" speech.) Later, during his presidency, Nixon borrowed money from wealthy friends to finance his San Clemente estate and was criticized for using government funds to improve his property. After his resignation, he was depleted financially until his appearance with David Frost in a series of television interviews and the publication of his memoirs.

Ferguson also borrowed money from wealthy friends and spent most of his life trying to get out of debt or get ahead. When he was 50, he wrote to his daughter that he didn't know if he would ever get out of debt at all, but he took solace in the fact that Jay Gould had gone broke and made his biggest fortune after he was 50.

The similarities are intriguing.

But of far more importance is the similarity between the Ferguson impeachment of 1917 and the Watergate Affair of 1972-74. After Richard Nixon's resignation, historians looked for parallels between Nixon's aborted impeachment and the impeachment of President Andrew Johnson. They found very few.

But the impeachment of Jim Ferguson offers compelling and uncanny parallels, and further, it offers some answers to the questions raised by the Watergate Affair. For instance, there are certain questions that puzzle legal scholars and theorists: What is an impeachable offense? Is impeachment a civil or a criminal proceeding? Is impeachment subject to judicial review? The failure to answer these questions correctly worked against Jim Ferguson and his counsel in 1917 and again in 1924; and they worked against Richard Nixon and his advisors in 1974. Indeed, if Richard Nixon's counselors had known about and understood the impeachment of Jim Ferguson, they might have avoided the same errors of judgment.

Impeachment is a political process more than a legal one, and neither Nixon nor Ferguson would have been impeached if events had not already eroded public confidence in them. As long as his political base is securely intact, no political official needs to worry about being impeached. But once the base is gone, because of public disenchantment, impeachment becomes a possibility.

Nixon's predicament became serious in 1973 when John Dean informed the Ervin Senate Committee in televised hearings that White House advisors had been involved in a cover-up of the Watergate story, and that former Attorney General John Mitchell had authorized the burglary of the National Democratic Headquarters in the Watergate Complex in Washington, D.C. Almost immediately, public confidence in Richard Nixon plummeted.

Similarly, Jim Ferguson's trouble began with a House investigation in March of 1917. The revelations of that investigation — that Ferguson had misused public funds and unduly influenced the officers of the bank he once owned, coercing them into loaning him excessive funds — turned many Texas voters against him.

Yet neither man was mortally wounded politically by the public hearings. Other events transpired to worsen their public standings.

Nixon was sued by the Watergate special prosecutor, Archibald Cox, to produce tape recordings of his White House conversations. Nixon responded by firing Cox and other officials (a debacle which became known as the Saturday Night Massacre), and almost at once, a cry went up from the press and figures in Congress for Nixon's impeachment or resignation.

In the same manner, when the Travis County Grand Jury indicted Jim Ferguson on criminal charges, Texas legislators immediately set out for Austin and began filling the Driskill Hotel.

If Nixon had not fired Archibald Cox and the other Justice Department officials, it is possible that he could have weathered the storm with his position intact. If Ferguson had not been indicted by the Travis County Grand Jury, the Texas legislature probably would not have convened in answer to the call of the speaker of the House.

What is an impeachable offense? Nixon and Ferguson both denigrated the charges brought against them, claiming that although they might have "made some mistakes," they had not committed impeachable offenses. But Nixon and Ferguson were both incorrect: They both committed impeachable offenses, a fact that is easily learned from a brief study of the history of impeachment.

Impeachment was first used by the English Parliament in the fourteenth century as a way of making ministers of the king answerable to Parliament for their misdeeds. The king might not care to correct or remove a minister, but Parliament would. Under the English system, the House of Commons prosecuted impeachments, and the House of Lords tried them; impeachments were usually punished by death. After the fourteenth century, the use of impeachment lapsed, as Parliament began to favor bills of attainder (legislative condemnations to death without a trial), but impeachment was again widely used in later centuries.

The foremost grounds for impeachment was treason, but treason in a special sense. Originally treason had meant disloyalty to the king—waging war against him or supporting his enemies — but often ministers were impeached for over-zealously carrying out the king's wishes. A minister might be very loyal to the king and yet still be impeached for treason, for treason came to denote "acts against the organic law of England."

Other than treason, grounds for impeachment became identified as "high crimes and misdemeanors," and it is this term that confused Richard Nixon and his advisors and Jim Ferguson and his counsel. They obviously believed that "high crimes" were crimes of a serious nature, such as murder or robbery.

In fact, "high crimes and misdemeanors" were offenses committed by persons of such rank or authority that they were beyond the ordinary reach of the law. The term itself is first found in English common law not in connection with a normal criminal proceeding but with an impeachment.

The transgressions that most commonly resulted in impeachment for "high crimes and misdemeanors" were misapplication of funds, mal-administration, rendering unconstitutional opinions, using high office to deny due process to individuals or to obtain personal gain, appointing unfit men, and neglect of duty in warfare.

Specific examples worth noting: The Earl of Suffolk was impeached in 1386 for misapplication of funds; the Duke of Suffolk in 1450 for appointing unfit men to office; Lord Middlesex in 1624 for allowing the office of ordnance to go unrepaid.

Against this background, it is clear that the charges against Jim Ferguson — misusing public funds, appointing friends to high office to serve his personal wishes, and tampering with the administration of state institutions — were clearly impeachable offenses. The same is true of the articles of impeachment adopted by the House Judiciary Committee against Richard Nixon. Both men in fact committed "high crimes and misdemeanors."

The Framers of the U.S. Constitution copied the English system (even though by then impeachment had become obsolete in England) and vested the power to bring impeachments in the House of Representatives and the power to try them in the Senate. And they borrowed also from the English system in setting out the grounds for impeachment — bribery, treason, and "high crimes and misdemeanors."

The American system differed from the English system in that the only punishment involved was removal from office. On this point, the Texas Constitution, although it copies the U.S. Constitution, is more like the old English one, for the Texas Senate could and did bar the impeached officer from holding office again.

In England, impeached ministers were not allowed to attend their impeachments or their trials, and in America impeached officials have generally chosen not to attend their impeachments: Andrew Johnson did not attend the proceedings against him in 1868. Jim Ferguson not only attended his impeachment and trial, but also dominated them with his testimony and speeches. Yet he probably would have faired better if he had not attended. Under the original English system, he would not have been allowed to do so.

Is impeachment a civil or a criminal proceeding?

The question is more than academic; in Texas, the answer that was reached was important in determining the rules of evidence and the admissibility of certain evidence. Further, anyone involved in legal proceeding has an interest in knowing just what it is. A defendant in a murder trial is clearly involved in a criminal proceeding, while a person involved in a divorce trial is just as certainly involved in a civil proceeding.

As for impeachment, it would seem that under the English system, it was a criminal proceeding, for surely it would be ludicrous for a civil trial to result in the death penalty for the defendant. But legal authorities generally agree that in America, where the only penalty is removal from office, it is not. It is seen as a political process and a tool for protecting the public from unfit officials; it is considered a "quasi-criminal" proceeding. As we have seen, this is the very conclusion that was reached by the president pro tem of the Texas Senate in 1917.

Is impeachment subject to judicial review?

The answer is no. In England, the House of Lords was the final authority in impeachments; there was no review possible. Certain kings sometimes pardoned impeached ministers, but those same kings sometimes found themselves at the gallows. Under the American system, there is likewise no judicial review possible; the Senate is the final authority.

Had Andrew Johnson or Richard Nixon been convicted by the Senate, no court could have restored either of them to office. Gerald Ford granted a pardon to Richard Nixon, but the pardon only prevented Nixon from being prosecuted in the courts for criminal offenses.

The case of Jim Ferguson is unique in that it enabled a court to determine that the judgment of the Texas Senate could not be overruled by a court. The Texas Supreme Court reached that decision in 1924, when it refused to allow Jim Ferguson's name to appear on the primary ballot, in defiance of the judgment of the High Court of Impeachment.

Other parallels between the Ferguson and Nixon affairs suggest themselves: The special prosecutors in the Watergate affair, Archibald Cox and then Leon Jaworski, played roles similar to the ones played by prosecutor M. M. Crane in 1917. And Gerald Ford and Will Hobby played similar parts: Both men inherited their offices from men who had been disgraced and proceeded to restore confidence in the integrity of their governments. President Ford returned a sense of honor and trust to the presidency, and Will Hobby re-established the integrity of the Texas governorship.

And finally, the case of Jim Ferguson offers some clues as to what would have happened to Richard Nixon if he had not resigned. Nixon claimed that the impeachment process in the Congress would take months, possibly even years, to conclude; he therefore resigned "for the good of the country."

Yet the impeachment of Jim Ferguson on more numerous charges required fewer than sixty days. It seems possible that the impeachment of Richard Nixon, prosecuted or managed perhaps by Leon Jaworski, would have been expedited by the introduction of testimony from Judge John Sirica's courtroom and the hearings of Senator Sam Ervin's committee.

The articles of impeachment were narrowly defined by the House Judiciary Committee, and Jaworski was intimately familiar with the Watergate case, just as M. M. Crane was thoroughly versed with the dealings of Jim Ferguson in 1917. Jaworski might have used the same tactics that Crane did, and relied on the testimony and witnesses that were already known and available to him. The impeachment of Richard Nixon might easily have been accomplished in the same sixty days or less that it took to convict Jim Ferguson.

Further, as this book is being written, Richard Nixon is still alive, and it should not be assumed that he will never again hold a high office. His political obituary has been delivered before. But a Republican president, such as Ronald Reagan, could conceivably appoint Richard Nixon to the Cabinet or to an ambassadorship. Impossible? It happened to Jim Ferguson.

8

Jim Ferguson and Lyndon Johnson: The Meaning of a Legend

When Lyndon Johnson graduated from high school in 1924, he set out for California with a group of friends in a Model T. He stayed in California for almost two years and held a variety of jobs: grapepicker, mechanic, dishwasher. Johnson's biographers as well as his friends consider this jaunt to the west coast as something of a lark, just a young man sowing some wild oats.

In fact, Lyndon Johnson's journey to California was a deliberate and seriously conceived act. For Lyndon Johnson was determined to follow in the footsteps of his idol, Farmer Jim Ferguson. Ferguson went to California when he was 16; Johnson when he was 17. Ferguson worked as a laborer and dishwasher, and so did Johnson. Ferguson returned home to Texas and took a job with the KATY Railroad; Johnson came home to take a job with a highway road gang. It was an important ritual for Johnson: he was emulating Farmer Jim.

The Ferguson influence on Lyndon Johnson's life began early, for Johnson's father, Sam Ealy Johnson was an ardent supporter of Farmer Jim.

Sam Johnson was a small farmer in Blanco County, Texas, until his brother-in-law, Clarence Martin, persuaded him to study law and then encouraged him to run for the Texas legislature, which Sam did, and served three terms in the Texas House of Representatives, from 1902 to 1908. Clarence Martin, of course, was one of Jim Ferguson's defense counsel and delivered closing arguments before the House and the High Court of Impeachment. (Some writers have identified Martin as Ferguson's chief defense counsel, but in fact he was an assistant to W. A. Hanger.)

Clarence Martin and Sam Johnson campaigned for Jim Ferguson throughout Blanco County in 1914 and again in 1918, and sometimes the boy Lyndon accompanied them on the campaign trail.

Lyndon was nine years old when Jim Ferguson was impeached, and the impeachment had a powerful impact on his family. The neighbor and relative Clarence Martin journeyed from Blanco County to serve as a Ferguson defender; and Sam Johnson decided to return to elective politics. Soon after the impeachment, a special election was held in Blanco County, and Sam ran for and was elected again to the state legislature. He got there too late to help save the Champion of the Tenant Farmer, but he would support Ferguson's campaigns for the Senate and the presidency. While serving in the House, Johnson supported and sponsored liberal legislation, and he fought against a 1918 loyalty bill that was based on anti-German sentiment in Texas. The bill set a prison sentence for using disloyal language.

Sam Johnson served in the legislature until 1924, and young Lyndon would attend the sessions with his father, sitting in the gallery, listening to the debates. And during this period, Johnson always accompanied his father on the campaign trail, including the campaign of 1922, when Sam Johnson and Jim Ferguson were both arguing against the Ku Klux Klan.

In 1927, Lyndon Johnson enrolled in Southwest Texas State Teachers College in San Marcos. His biographers have said that he chose Southwest Texas over the nearby University of Texas because he wanted to attend a smaller school. In fact, given the role that the University of Texas played in the impeachment of Jim Ferguson, Lyndon Johnson would have gone to college anyplace except that university.

In 1931, Johnson went to Washington as a secretary to Texas Congressman Richard Kleberg and thus launched his political career. From that point on, he would have other mentors, including Texas Senator Sam Rayburn and President Franklin

Roosevelt, but the Ferguson influence on his life would continue.

In 1932, Miriam Ferguson, having been defeated for re-election bids in 1926 and 1930, was again elected governor of Texas. In 1933, while banks across the country were failing daily, President Roosevelt ordered a banking moratorium, and closed all the banks in America for seven days. In Texas, Governor Ma Ferguson pre-empted the President by declaring a moratorium before Roosevelt did, her moratorium to coincide with his but lasting for thirteen days. Later, during this same term, Mrs. Ferguson won passage of $20 million bond issue to raise money to feed the destitute; the bonds being known as "Bread Bonds." Lyndon Johnson never forgot the role that the Fergusons played in fighting the Depression in Texas.

Johnson himself had a hand in fighting that Depression. Appointed to serve as Texas Director of the National Youth Association in 1935, Johnson distributed New Deal dollars to Texas students who would stay in school.

The Depression had dealt a hardship to students and school enrollments dropped drastically. In Temple, Texas, investigators for the school district found that students who missed school did so usually because they either did not have shoes to wear in cold weather, or they did not have food to take with them for lunch.

Johnson later rose to power in Washington, as a congressman, senator and Senate Majority Leader. Along the way, though, he lost one election, a special senatorial election held in Texas in 1941 to fill the seat of U.S. Senator Morris Sheppard, who had died in office. Jim Ferguson supported Johnson's opponent, Governor Pappy O'Daniel, and in a razor close election, O'Daniel defeated Johnson. Johnson's supporters urged him to demand a recount, but he refused.

Three years later, in 1944, Jim Ferguson, Old Jim, as they called him then, lay dying, and Lyndon Johnson went to be with him. He called on the Fergusons and stayed by Old Jim's death bed. Ferguson's daughter was impressed by that, and wrote about it in the biography of her parents.

Lyndon Johnson was too big a man to hold a grudge, she said. While Jim was dying, Johnson was his most frequent caller. Of course Lyndon Johnson didn't hold a grudge against Old Jim; after all, he had first been on the campaign trail for Ferguson when he was six years old. His father loved Jim Ferguson, and Lyndon loved Jim Ferguson. His childhood had been spent in the aura of the Champion of the Tenant Farmer. He idolized Ferguson and modeled himself after Jim. This can be seen in several ways, beginning with that journey to California when Johnson got out of high school.

Jim Ferguson was more than just a popular Texas politician: He was a folk hero, a legendary figure. The legend he personified is this: the legend of a poor boy who would rise from the land to enter the halls of power to work for the poor and the oppressed, to use his eloquence and persuasiveness to argue for the rights of the common people. "I have remembered the poor boys and the poor girls," Jim Ferguson told the High Court of Impeachment, "and I have worked to help them." Which explains the tenant farm law and the $2 million appropriation for the rural schools and the Bread Bonds.

It is the legend of a man who would never quit, who would always come back from defeat to claim victory for the people. It is the legend of a man of the people who would be fearless and persevering. Jim Ferguson ran alone and unafraid against the Ku Klux Klan in 1922, and Lyndon Johnson never forgot it. Ferguson lost that year, but he came back two years later to run the Klan out of Texas politics, and Johnson never forgot that, either.

It is the legend of a man who never broke his word. He promised to pass a tenant farm bill, and he did; he promised to pass an anti-mask law, and he did; he promised that he would never tell who had loaned him the $156,000, even if it cost him his office, and he never told.

In his day, Lyndon Johnson would work to personify the same legend. Did Ferguson work for the poor? Through his Great Society programs, Johnson fought a war against poverty. Did Ferguson work for the rural schools? As president, Johnson tried to make it possible for every child in America to obtain a college education. Did Ferguson deal a death blow to the Ku

Klux Klan with the anti-mask law? With the Civil Rights Act of 1964, Johnson tried to eliminate racial discrimination forever.

Lyndon Johnson's various biographers have yet to deal with the great influence that Jim Ferguson had on his life. Even though Johnson tried to tell them about Ferguson, they have dealt with the matter only in passing. But some day, a biographer will deal more fully with Johnson and Ferguson.

Johnson often spoke about Ferguson, even to those who were writing books about the president, both while he was in the White House and after he had retired. But the writers didn't know the legend of Farmer Jim and so didn't understand what Lyndon Johnson was trying to tell them.

NOTES

1

The Call of the Speaker

Fuller's call for a special session is reported in the *Temple Daily Telegram*, July 24, 1917. The proceedings of the House investigation in March were published as a book, *Investigation of the Hon. Jas. E. Ferguson*, Austin 1917. Ferguson's war with the University of Texas is covered in detail by Ralph W. Steen in "Jim Ferguson's War on the University of Texas," *Southwest Social Science Quarterly*, Spring, 1954.

The protest march by the University of Texas students is reported in the *Temple Daily Telegram*, May 29, 1917, and discussed in detail by Lewis H. Gould in *Progressives and Prohibitionists: Texas Democrats in the Age of Wilson*, Austin, 1974.

Ferguson's meeting with Fuller on the locating matter is based on both men's testimony before the Texas House of Representatives, described in Chapter Three.

Ferguson's speech to the State Farmers Institute is from the *Temple Daily Telegram*, July 27, 1917. That same issue describes the position statement issued by the conference of lawyers in Austin.

Ferguson's indictment by the Travis County Grand Jury is covered in the *Temple Daily Telegram*, July 28, 1917, as is the serving of process papers, Ferguson's message to the press and the position issued by the Texas Attorney General.

Will Hogg's role in precipitating the impeachment is discussed by Gould in *Progressives and Prohibitionists*.

Ferguson's speech in Walnut Springs is taken from the *Temple Daily Telegram*, July 29, 1917. Longtime Texas Congressman Bob Poage remembers Ferguson's supporters often shouting, "Pour it on 'em, Jim!" The silence of the crowd is noticed in the *Temple Daily Telegram*. The same issue describes the phone manager accepting the Army commission and legislators filling the Driskill Hotel.

Ferguson's call for a special session is from the *Temple Daily Telegram*, July 31, 1917.

Fuller's introduction of the charges is from the *Temple Daily Telegram*, August 2, 1917, as is Ferguson's message to the press.

The background information on M. M. Crane is from *Who's Who in America*. The background information on W. A. Hanger is from *History of Texas, Volume Three*, edited by Captain B. B. Craddock, Chicago, 1922, and the *Fort Worth Star-Telegram*, September 29, 1940.

Hanger's alma mater, Cumberland Law School, provided more U.S. Congressmen than any other institution in America in the nineteenth century, according to *History of Wilson County, Tennessee*, edited by Dixon Merritt, Lebanon, Tennessee, 1961.

2

The Unknown Ferguson

Jim Ferguson's early life is based primarily on the family biography by his daughter, Ouida — *The Fergusons of Texas* by Ouida Ferguson Nalle, San Antonio, 1946.

The history of Bell County is based on George W. Tyler's *History of Bell County, Texas,* San Antonio, 1936. (The book was edited by Charles W. Ramsdell and published after the author's death. It was probably completed by 1920.)

3

The Proceedings of the House

The proceedings of the Texas House of Representatives are based on the recrd of the proceedings in the *Temple Daily Telegram,* August 6 — August 29, 1917. The record of the proceedings were published in a book; comparison confirms the accuracy of the record in the *Temple Daily Telegram.* This applies to the sequence of witnesses, the testimony, the speeches, etc.

Hobby's meeting with Ferguson to take over the responsibilities of the governor's office is described by James A. Clark and Weldon Hart in *The Tactful Texan: A Biography of Governor Will Hobby,* New York, 1958.

The Houston race riot is described in the *Temple Daily Telegram,* August 24, 1917. The pardons Ferguson issued at the last minute are from the TDT, August 25, 1917.

4

The High Court of Impeachment

The Senate phone call to John Nelson Phillips is from the *Temple Daily Telegram,* August 27, 1917. Ferguson's refund to the state is from the TDT, August 28, 1917.

The vote of the Senate on the appointment to the Board of Regents is from the *Temple Daily Telegram,* August 29, 1917.

The record of the proceedings of the Texas Senate sitting as a High Court of Impeachment is based on the record of the trial in the *Temple Daily Telegram,* September 4–September 24, 1917. The record of the trial is available in book form; a comparison confirms the accuracy of the record in the *Temple Daily Telegram,.*

Ferguson's open letter to the people of Texas is from the *Temple Daily Telegram,* September 3, 1917.

Gene Van Gent, the Longhorn football coach, leaving the University of Texas campus along with his players to enlist in the American Army is from Lou Maysel, *Here Come the Texas Longhorns,* Fort Worth, Texas, 1970.

5

The Acting Governor

There are several accounts of Will Hobby's governorship of Texas. This study relies heavily on Clark and Hart's *The Tactful Texan* and Gould's *Progressives and Prohibitionists.*

6

Jim Ferguson and the Ku Klux Klan

John Lomax's career as a folk song collector is recounted in his memoir, *Confessions of a Ballad Hunter,* New York, 1947.

The Ferguson-Hobby 1918 campaign for the Texas governorship is reported by Clark and Hart in *The Tactful Texan* as well as by Gould in *Progressives and Prohibitionists.*

The Internal Revenue Service's revelation that Ferguson's infamous loan had come from Texas brewers is reported by Clark and Hart, and also Gould.

The history of the Ku Klux Klan, including the tokens and nomenclature of Klankraft are based on Charles C. Alexander's *Crusade for Conformity: The Ku Klux Klan in Texas 1920-1930,* Houston 1962.

The Maddox suit is reported in the *Temple Daily Telegram,* May 16, 1924. The legal record of the case can be found in the *Southwestern Reporter 283.* The decision to omit Ferguson's name from the ballot is reported in the *Temple Daily Telegram,* May 18, 1924. W. G. Love's appeal of the case, as well as Miriam Ferguson's application to be certified as a candidate for governor, are from the TDT, May 30, 1924. A full discussion of the Maddox suit and the implications of the Ferguson case for American law can be found in Wilbourn E. Benton's *Texas: Its Government and Politics,* Englewood Cliffs, New Jersey, 1961. (Numerous editions have since been published.)

Ferguson's speech in Copperas Cove is from the *Temple Daily Telegram,* June 15, 1924; the Klan induction ceremony in Temple is reported in the TDT, July 8, 1924.

Robertson's speech, "I am the man the Ku Klux Klan endorsed . . . " is from Alexander, *Crusade for Conformity.*

Ferguson's speeches in Dallas and Waco are from next-day reports in the *Temple Daily Telegram;* Robertson's speech in Temple is reported in the TDT, August 13, 1924. Ferguson's prediction of victory is from the TDT, August 23, 1924.

Professor Butte's late entry into the campaign is described by Ferguson's daughter in *The Fergusons of Texas,* and by Clark and Hart; and also Gould.

A discussion of Miriam Ferguson's "co-governorship" and her voice in the affairs of Texas can be found in a book by Fred Gantt, Jr., *The Chief Executive in Texas: A Study in Executive Leadership,* Austin, 1964.

Miriam Ferguson's appointment of three women to sit as special justices on the Texas Supreme Court is based on a photograph in *Texas Jurists 1836-1936*, Austin, 1937.

The Ku Klux Klan's last Klorero in Temple is taken from Alexander's *Crusade for Conformity*.

7

Jim Ferguson and Richard Nixon:
The Constitutional Questions

There are many biographical works on Richard Nixon. This study relies on *Nixon vs. Nixon* by David Abrahamsen, New York, 1976.

The history of impeachment is based on Raoul Berger's *Impeachment: The Constitutional Questions,* Cambridge, Massachusettes, 1973. Berger offers the best analysis of "high crimes and misdemeanors" as well as impeachable offenses.

The significance of the Ferguson case in the law of impeachment is analyzed by Benton in *Texas: Its Government and Politics.*

There are many works on the Watergate case and the aborted impeachment of Richard Nixon. This work relies on *The Right and the Power* by Leon Jaworski, New York, 1976, and *The Final Days* by Bob Woodward and Carl Bernstein, New York, 1976.

8

Jim Ferguson and Lyndon Johnson:
The Meaning of a Legend

Lyndon Johnson's journey to California is discussed in many works, including Doris Kearns' *Lyndon Johnson and the American Dream,* New York, 1976.

Sam Johnson's life and the influence Clarence Martin had on it are described in *Lyndon Johnson: The Formative Years* by William Pool, Emmie Craddock, and David E. Conrad, San Marcos, Texas, 1965.

Lyndon Johnson and his father campaigning for Jim Ferguson is discussed in most of the Johnson biographies, especially by Alfred Steinberg in *Sam Johnson's Boy,* New York, 1968.

Miriam Ferguson's "Bread Bonds" are discussed in Gantt's *The Chief Executive in Texas.*

The affect of the Great Depression on Ferguson's old hometown is described in a thesis by Robert Allan Ozment, *Temple, Texas, and the Great Depression,* Austin, 1966.

Eric F. Goldman had some idea of the great influence of Jim Ferguson on Lyndon Johnson. Listening to Johnson discuss his ideas for fighting poverty and advancing education, Goldman said, "This was the voice of Old Jim . . . " — Eric F. Goldman, *The Tragedy of Lyndon Johnson,* New York, 1969.

BIBLIOGRAPHY

David Abrahamsen
Nixon vs. Nixon
Farrar, Straus and Giroux
New York, 1976.

Charles C. Alexander
Crusade for Conformity: The Ku Klux Klan in Texas 1920-1930
Texas Gulf Coast Historical Association
Houston, 1962

Wilbourn E. Benton
Texas: Its Government and Politics
Prentice-Hall
Englewood Cliffs, N.J., 1961

Raoul Berger
Impeachment: The Constitutional Questions
Harvard University Press
Cambridge, Mass., 1973

Capt. B. B. Braddock, editor
History of Texas, Volume III
Lewis Publishing Company
Chicago, 1922

Eldon Stephen Branda, editor
The Handbook of Texas, Volume 3
Texas State Historical Association
Austin, 1976

James A. Clark, with Weldon Hart
The Tactful Texan: A Biography of Governor Will Hobby
Randon House
New York, 1958

Fred Gantt, Jr.
The Chief Executive in Texas: A Study in Executive Leadership
University of Texas Press
Austin, 1964

Eric F. Goldman
The Tragedy of Lyndon Johnson
Alfred A. Knopf
New York, 1969

Lewis H. Gould
Progressive and Prohibitionists: Texas Democrats in the Age of Wilson
University of Texas Press
Austin, 1974

Leon Jaworski
The Right and the Power
Reader's Digest / Gulf
New York, 1976

Doris Kearns
Lyndon Johnson and the American Dream
Harper and Row
New York, 1976

John A. Lomax
Adventures of a Ballad Hunter
Macmillan
New York, 1947

Lou Maysel
Here Come the Texas Longhorns
Stadium Publishing Company
Fort Worth, 1970

Ouida Ferguson Nalle
The Fergusons of Texas
Naylor
San Antonio, 1946
The author is Jim Ferguson's daughter

Robert Allan Ozment
Temple, Texas, and the Great Depression
M.A. Thesis, University of Texas
Austin, 1966

W. R. "Bob" Poage
Politics Texas Style
Privately Published
Waco, Texas, 1976

William C. Pool, Emmie Craddock, and David E. Conrad
Lyndon Johnson, The Formative Years
Southwest Texas State College Press
San Marcos, Texas, 1965

Alfred Steinberg
Sam Johnson's Boy
Macmillan
New York, 1968

George W. Tyler
A History of Bell County, Texas
Naylor
San Antonio, 1936
Edited by Charles W. Ramsdell and published after the author's death.
Completed about 1920.

Walter Prescott Webb, editor
The Handbook of Texas Two Volumes
Texas State Historical Association
Austin, 1952

Bob Woodward and Carl Bernstein
The Final Days
Simon and Schuster
New York, 1976

INDEX

Allen, Wilbur P., 12, 28, 29, 41, 42, 53, 69, 91, 93, 95, 109
Allred, James, 14
Anti-Mask Law, 20, 145
Axton, Stockton, 42, 60

Bartlett, Churchill J., 113
Bell, Peter Hansborough, 15
Blum, Henry, 23, 25, 26, 27, 31, 32, 74, 75, 76
Brackenridge, George W., 71
Brents, W. R., 79, 80
Bryan, Charles W., 129
    E. R., 61, 62
Butte, George C., 131

Canyon City Normal College, 5, 6, 10, 45, 56, 64, 68, 69, 85, 88, 90, 92, 96, 104, 105, 107, 108, 109
"Chicken salad case," 26, 61, 87-87, 88, 100
Colquitt, Oscar B., 5, 26, 43, 45
Connerly, Fred, 26
Coolidge, Calvin, 128
Cooper, O. H., 41
Cox, Archibald, 135, 136, 139
Cox, B. A., 28
Crane, M. M., viii, 13, 14, 22, 23, 25, 26, 27, 28, 29, 30, 31, 32, 33, 39, 42, 43, 47, 55, 56, 58, 59, 60, 61, 62, 63, 72, 73, 74, 75, 76, 77, 78, 79, 80, 81, 82, 84, 86, 87, 88, 89, 90, 96, 98, 99, 100, 101, 102, 104, 106, 107, 108, 125, 139
Cumberland College, 13-14, 44
Cummings, B. Y., 65, 102

Davidson, Lynch, 128, 129
Davis, Fred W., 32, 34
    James W., 129

J. H., 27, 31, 45, 57, 74, 89-92, 97, 100
Dean, John, 135
Dean, W. L., 73, 77, 86, 87, 91
Downs, P. L., 28, 79
Dubose, Clarence, 85

Edwards, Jim, 26
Eisenhower, Dwight D., 120
Ervin, Sam, 135, 139
Evans, Hiram Wesley, 124, 125

Ferguson, A. F., 27, 92
    James Eldridge, 17-18
    Miriam Amanda, vii, 19, 20, 21, 126, 128, 129, 130, 131, 134, 143
    Wesley, 19
Ford, Gerald, 133, 138, 139
Fox, Henry, 27, 76, 89, 92
Frost, David, 134
Fuller, F. O., 1, 2, 4, 5, 9, 12, 23, 32, 33, 34, 35, 37, 38, 39, 41, 43, 52, 53, 54, 63, 64, 65, 66, 110

Gould, Jay, 134
Gross, F. A., 85, 86

Hancock, Curyiss, 33, 79, 94
Hanger, W. A., viii, 13, 14, 23, 25, 26, 30, 31, 32, 33, 34, 37, 38, 40, 41, 43, 44, 45, 46, 47, 50, 51, 52, 54, 55, 59, 63, 64, 73, 74, 75, 76, 77, 78, 80, 81, 83, 85, 86, 87, 88, 89, 91, 92, 96, 97, 102, 125, 142
Harrell, Will, 51
Hargon, Frank, 89
Harris, Will, 102
Heard, T. H., 46, 65, 76, 94
Henry, Bob, 78

Hobby, Oveta Culp, 120
  Will, 2, 4, 24, 32, 35, 51, 52,
    69, 70, 71, 94, 108, 114,
    115, 116, 117, 118, 119,
    121, 123, 139
  Will, Jr., 120
Hogg, James Stephen, 6, 13
  Will, 6, 34, 41, 51, 65
Hughes, C. A., 45
Hutchins, Adjutant General, 39

Jaworski, Leon, 139
Johnson, Andrew, 43, 134, 138
  Lyndon, viii, 14, 141, 142, 143,
    144, 145
  Sam Ealy, 14, 141, 142
Jones, S. J., 28

Kleberg, Richard, 142
Ku Klux Klan, vii, 20, 95, 103, 122,
    123, 124, 127, 128, 129,
    130, 131, 132, 134, 142,
    144, 145

Lattimore, O. S., 101
Lee, T. P., 131
Lomax, John A., 29, 42, 95, 121
Looney, Ben, 6, 34
Love, W. G., 126

Martin, Clarence, 64, 66, 102, 141,
    142
Mansfield, H. P., 84, 89
Mayfield, Earl B., 123, 124
McAdoo, William Gibbs, 129
McCall, John D., 28, 70
McFarland, M. M., 40-41
Mitchell, John, 135

Nalle, Ouida (Ferguson), 18, 133
Nixon, Julie, 133
  Richard, viii, 133, 134, 135,
    136, 137, 138, 139, 140

O'Daniel, W. Lee ("Pappy"), 143

Petty, George, 105
Phillips, John Nelson, 16, 24, 71, 73
Porter, William Sidney (O. Henry),
    115

Rayburn, Sam, 142
Reagan, Ronald, 140
Robertson, Felix D., 125, 128, 129,
    130
Roosevelt, Franklin D., 142-43

Salado College, 17, 133
Saunders, X. B., 17, 18, 19
Sheppard, Morris, 143
Simmons, William Joseph, 124, 125
Sirica, John, 139
Smith, Al, 128, 129
  Howard K., 134
Sterling, R. S., 84
Sulzer, William, 73
Swor, Frank, 28, 96

Tenant Farm Law, 8
Terrell, Chester, 32, 34, 39, 40, 62,
    64, 65, 86
Texas, University of, 1, 2, 4, 7, 9, 12,
    18, 29, 31, 46, 47, 48, 49,
    77, 79, 82, 94, 95, 99,
    111, 117, 119
Thommason, W. E., 40, 51, 64
Turner, A. A., 86

Van Gent, Gene, 83
Vinson, Robert E., 2, 29, 30, 31, 42,
    48, 50, 51, 60, 79, 80, 81,
    82, 83, 84, 93

Ward, Hortense, 131
West Texas A. and M. University, 2,
    9, 32, 35, 51, 68
Whittiere College, 133
Widen, Carl, 33-34, 77
Wilson, Woodrow, 42, 60, 118
Woodman, C. W., 11, 28, 53, 69,
    111